The Untold History of Canada

THE TRAGIC

CONSEQUENCES

OF THE QUEBEC

ACT OF 1774

By Pierre Beaudry

With a forward by Matthew Ehret and
Appendix by Lyndon H. LaRouche Jr.

Matthew Ehret
www.canadianpatriot.org

Printed in Canada

First Printing: December 2018
Canadian Patriot Press

KDP ISBN- 9781792731235
Print Edition

The painting on the cover features Benjamin Franklin, who was celebrated as the "Prometheus of America" for his discovery of electricity and defiance of the Zeusian principle while organizing the American revolution. The painting was rendered by Franklin's friend, American painter Benjamin West.

SHORT AFFILIATION BIOGRAPHY OF PIERRE BEAUDRY

Pierre Beaudry is a retired researcher for Executive Intelligence Review (EIR) headquartered in Leesburg Virginia, USA. Formerly Professor at the University of Montreal, he has been an associate of American economist Lyndon LaRouche since 1974. His principal written contributions in the domains of Classical Artistic Composition, Epistemology, Geometry, and History can be found in Pierre Beaudry's Galactic Parking Lot (www.amatterofmind.org).

For further information contact pierrebeaudry@amatterofmind.org

CONTENTS

FORWARD BY MATTHEW EHRET

Some Words About "The Untold History of Canada" Series

"The state itself is never the purpose, it is important only as the condition under which the purpose of mankind may be fulfilled, and this purpose of mankind is none other than the development of all the powers of people, i.e., progress. If the constitution of a state hinders the progress of the mind, it is contemptible and harmful, however well thought-out it may otherwise be... In general, we can establish a rule for judging political institutions, that they are only good and laudable, to the extent that they bring all forces inherent in persons to flourish, to the extent that they promote the progress of culture, or at least not hinder it. This rule applies to religious laws as well as to political ones: both are contemptible if they constrain a power of the human mind, if they impose upon the mind any sort of stagnation."

-Frederick Schiller, poet, dramatist and founder of the Science of Universal History, excerpted from his lecture on the Constitutions of Lycurgus' Sparta and Solon's Athens

I can only imagine that as you pick up this book which is part of the "Untold History of Canada" series you may be asking yourself, *"well this author seems to be saying that they know something which they profess to be true and new about Canada... but how could anything new be said of a subject which has been dissected and chronicled by hundreds of thousands of authors for over 150 years? How is it possible that historical truths can even be known when history books are invariably written by the winners? What makes this version of Canada's history so different from everything that came before?"*

In answering these questions, I say that if we only had history books to work with, then the answer to the first question would be a definitive "No. Truth could thus be known in history". However, if we recognize that history is not a mere collection of facts in books, but is rather a *process* shaped by individual personalities motivated by IDEAS of humanity and nature which are either right or wrong, and if these individuals played driving roles in the unfolding of history, then certainly we have much more than text books to work with.

In the course of human history, certain singular periods jump out from the monotonous flow of day to day events. At times of crisis, patterns of behaviour, norms and customs no longer work, systems break down and the civilization in question either transforms to something new and better, or collapses into what some have called dark ages.

Should a transformation to something better occur, then we will often discover that such a society was fortunate enough that a prophet had appeared among them. Such a prophet, though often hated and misunderstood in his own lifetime, will often provide the creative energy, leadership and cognitive dissonance necessary to break that society out of its complacency and free from the doomed pattern of behaviour which only served to perpetuate the social structures of an encrusted elite on the one hand while rendering the lives of the masses useless on the other.

Examples of such prophets and poets shine as beacons of light in a dark abyss, whose lives we can say in hindsight were completely necessary for the continuity of society's collective evolution. From Socrates and his student Plato who founded an academy dedicated to the perfectibility of mankind in Ancient Athens, to Confucius and his student Mencius who did the same in China, it matters not from what particular civilization these individuals arise, the cultural force they represent is universal and thus transcends all particulars.

This principle is expressed in the impassioned poetry of Aeschylus, whose Prometheus Bound remains one of the clearest expositions to this day of the Christian power of agapic love which gives the heart the courage and the mind the self-discipline required to stand defiant against the tyrannical will of Zeus' law which posits that mankind remain as ignorant as the beasts, never to learn the secrets of the fire that is symbolic for his own creative potentiality.

It was this Promethean fire that burned in the heart of Augustine of Hippo as he arose to the stage of history and challenged the oligarchical priesthood of Rome that was trying desperately to sink a newly emerging Christian world back into the pagan sophistry of empire. Its heat was felt again vividly in the person of Dante Alighieri who opposed the will of Venice when he revolutionized literature and the Italian language, creating the conditions for the later Italian Renaissance to blossom in the 15th century. In spite of the efforts of such Prometheans as Joan of Arc, King Louis the XI or Cardinal Mazarin and Jean Baptiste Colbert of France who led the 1648 Peace of Westphalia- the corruption wrought by Zeus in Europe had poisoned the culture too well for the fires to properly take hold.

Amidst this demoralizing European decay of the 17th century, a new seat of fire abounding with ripe kindling was found an ocean away.

The seeds for humanity's rebirth appeared thus on the shores of a small colony known as New England, led by John Winthrop. This was the Winthrop who said during his inauguration of the Massachusetts Bay Colony in 1630; *"We shall be as a city upon a hill, the eyes of all people are upon us."*

Indeed the eyes of the world were upon them, as the hopes for a durable republican civilization dreamt of by Plato two millennia earlier could possibly finally take root. The early decades of this government bestowed with an independent charter founded explicitly upon the welfare of the governed, saw remarkable success. It had witnessed the issuance of the first colonial scrip to finance the industrial growth of the Sawguss Iron works and many internal improvements which led to a dramatic leap in the standards of living and cognitive powers of its people beyond anything seen in Europe. The cultural fire and taste for liberty grew fervently through this process and in spite of a desperate attempt on the part of Venetian puppets newly installed in England to stifle this fire in 1688, it continued to burn and the fight continued.

By the early 18th century, the leading Promethean in America who carried on John Winthrop's vision was a young disciple of Cotton Mather whose name was Benjamin Franklin.

Over the course of his entire life, this young man internalized the most universal lessons available to a creative mind and shaped himself patiently for a battle he knew was to come. Along the way, Franklin single-handedly sculpted a culture capable of internalizing and adding to the most profound ideas concerning man and nature then available.

Franklin's discovery of the principle of electricity shocked the world earning him the reputation among European humanists as the

"Prometheus of America" who stole fire from the Gods and gave it to man. Most of the European elite were perplexed that a commoner from the land of barbarians on the outskirts of the Empire could possibly trump the greatest minds of Europe. What's more- they could not comprehend how Franklin's discovery of the universal principle of electricity was intertwined with his understanding of the universal principle of creative thought. After all, were one not made in the others' image, and if the microcosm (mind) not a reflection of the macrocosm (universe), then a discovery of principle such as he made, could never occur!

Most importantly, Franklin and his international co-thinkers of scientists, poets and statesmen also recognized that without *political freedom* those natural powers of creative reason which all humanity share in kinship and are the basis of our inalienable rights- can never be actualized. It is this essence of Natural Law which inspired Franklin to shape the leadership that later came to be known as the founding fathers of America.

The inability of all Zeus-minded elite to conceive of the unified relationship between moral and scientific law has always been the greatest blind spot of empire. History teaches us that any ruling power which believes it must crush freedom and creativity in the souls of those it wishes to rule in order to maintain what it perceives to be its self-interest, will always be self-doomed as the parasite which can only kill the host upon which its survival depends. Contemplating this phenomenon American poet Edgar Poe once famously stated; one may convince a bird that its nature is to creep and crawl like a worm, but that will only lead to a tortured and slow death since its nature has always been to soar.

The life's deeds and original writings of such keystone Private Prometheans as Plato, Confucius, Augustine, Dante, Franklin et al remain invaluable resources for any who care to seek. Inversely, leading spokesman representing the oligarchical worldview also lived, acted and wrote their thoughts which are also widely available for any researcher (sadly more available than those writings of the aforementioned humanists).

But this only leaves one of our two questions answered. What about the second portion? What makes this version of Canada's "untold history" more truthful than anything else that came before it?

To begin with, no book on Canada that this author has ever encountered takes on the subject from the CONTEXT of universal history, and none have recognized that there can be no truthful history of Canada without taking into effect the dynamic of all world history as a battle of ideas.

I am convinced that it is by understanding this universal battle over ideas as it existed in Benjamin Franklin's mind, while observing his role in universal history, and his efforts to bring a young French colony named Quebec into this historical battle that the greatest insight into the paradox that is Canada can be gleamed.

When we observe that this dynamic of Universal history expressed by the Prometheus vs Zeus worldviews was at the heart of the American colonies' break from the British Empire, and as we identify this break as the single most important phenomenon of modern world history, then and only then, can a lawful understanding of Canada be grasped.

Just as our character in life is formed by the decisions we take (or fail to take) while we are alive, so too is the character of a nation formed. And by failing to accept the challenge of becoming the 14th colony to declare independence in 1776, a distorted anti-Promethean principle became implanted in our collective experience as a people in 1791, then again with the Act of Union of 1840, and again with the British North American Act of 1867 and yet again with the rise of "new nationalism" in

1963. While Promethean tendencies, being the natural state of humanity, have undoubtedly arisen from time to time in Canada's experience, it has too often occurred in a confused form. Never self-consciously as we have seen it manifest in such figures as Franklin, George Washington, Alexander Hamilton, William Gilpin, or Abraham Lincoln later.

While good Canadian intentions and creative efforts have contributed much prosperity and progress which we must cherish and celebrate, it must be recognized that more often than not, the inability of most Canadians, motivated by Promethean impulses, to reconcile those irreconcilable principles of monarchism and republicanism have led them to make tragic errors, thus undoing much of the good that they yearned to accomplish. This was clearly seen in the failed attempts by William Lyon Mackenzie and Louis Joseph Papineau to conduct their republican revolutions in 1837-38, in Sir Wilfred Laurier's attempts to create a customs union of the America's in 1911, Prime Minister William Mackenzie King's desires to construct a just post-war world and John Diefenbaker's failure to accomplish his Northern Vision in 1963.

When one begins to tune one's mind to looking at history from the standpoint of IDEAS of the future that should have been, rather than merely charting what came to pass as modern chroniclers are wont to do, may we then begin to explore history from a truthful standpoint.

Benjamin Franklin: Canadian Nation-builder

Canada Post

Benjamin Frankin was not only busy shaping the American revolution, but played a guiding role in shaping Canada's most valuable institutions including the Postal Service (250 year commemorative stamp featured on left) and the Montreal Gazette as the first Canadian newspaper featured below alongside french republican editor Fleury Mesplat whom Franklin brought in from France to found it. Pictures of an early Gazette and the Letter to the Inhabitants of Quebec calling on the Quebecois to become the 14th colony to declare independence published by Mesplat are also featured.

All paintings from Wiki Commons

CHAPTER I - THE TRAGIC CONSEQUENCES OF THE QUEBEC ACT OF 1774

From the standpoint of American military strategy, the invasion of Canada, a year before the Declaration of Independence, had two definite goals. Firstly, the purpose was to defeat the British army and make Canada the 14th colony of the United States and secondly, to preempt a British invasion of the American colonies from the north. George Washington had been explicit in his orders to Major General Richard Montgomery, the American leader of the Canada expedition. This mission was to take the two main cities of Montreal and of Quebec City and put them under the banner of the American colonies.

The first objective of the invasion failed and the tragic consequences of not having given the Canadians a true liberation are still being felt to this day. The reason for the failure is not to be found entirely in the treasonous activities of a few Americans, but primarily, in the Quebec Act of 1774, an "Intolerable Act" as the Americans stated it in their own Declaration of Independence. The evil of this Quebec Act succeeded in turning the French Canadians into a little people that preferred to support the continued rule of the British oligarchy and their deeply rooted moral corruption.

The Intolerable Acts

American revolutionaries considered the Quebec Act as an Intolerable Act because it was part of a series of coercive or punitive measures that the British Parliament had taken up, at the instigation of the British East India Company, during the period following the Treaty of Paris of 1763, for the purpose of provoking war against the thirteen American colonies. It is essential that the Quebec Act of 1774 be understood in the context of a whole series of Acts pronounced by the Parliament of Britain against the American colonies during that same year.

For example, on March 31, 1774, the Parliament of Great Britain passed a measure in response to the Boston Tea Party called the American Boston Port Act, outlawing the use of the Port of Boston, as a punitive measure against the colonists of Massachusetts. As the port of Boston served as a major business facility for all shipping goods all the way to South Carolina, the closing of its trade became one of the causes that unified the thirteen colonies. Then, the British Parliament passed the Massachusetts Government Act, on May 20, 1774, for the purpose of stopping the revolutionary ferment in the Massachusetts Bay Colony, by giving the British the right to nominate a governor of their choice. Other intolerable Acts were passed such as the Administration of Justice Act (May 20, 1774) also giving the British the right to replace the local American judicial system by British law. The Quartering Act, passed earlier on March 14, 1765, required that Americans let British soldiers stay in their homes.

The Quebec Act of 1774, in appearance unrelated to the American colonies, gave the British the right to expand the territory of Quebec into Ontario and Indian territories, as well as into lands that included Illinois, Indiana, Michigan, Ohio, Wisconsin and parts of Minnesota. Such an "Intolerable Act" represented not only a strategic danger for the thirteen colonies but was instrumental in leading them to institute their first Continental Congress and make their Declaration of Independence. In point of fact, the American Declaration of Independence referenced all of these "Intolerable Acts" including the Quebec Act, itself, as being the fundamental reason to "dissolve their political bands" with Britain on July 4, 1776.

In the case of Quebec, the Declaration explicitly denounced Britain *"For abolishing the free System of English Laws in a neighbouring Province, establishing therein an Arbitrary government, and enlarging its Boundaries as to render it at once an example and fit instrument for introducing the same absolute rule into these Colonies."*[1] This section of the Declaration of Independence was made in direct reference to the Quebec Act of 1774.

The Aftermath of the Treaty of Paris of 1763

From the same strategic standpoint, the British Empire knew they were going to have a war against the American colonies at least as early as 1745, after the siege of Louisburg and, therefore, had to secure the continent of America well before 1776. The necessity to prepare for the inevitable was the true motive behind the Seven-Years War with France and Spain. The British aim was to seize Canada from the French and Florida from the Spanish, and establish the British East India Company under Prince Rupert's authority in Canada. To this day, historians of the Treaty of Paris of 1763 wonder why the British chose to negotiate Canada instead of the French West Indies. This silly shortsightedness was caused by comparing the uneven commercial values between fur and rum. When Canada is viewed strategically as a flank against the United States, then, the choice becomes clear. So, it was only at the end of the Seven-Years War, in 1763, that the British East India Company considered they were ready for a war against the American colonies, and not before. And that is the reason why the British instituted systematically a series of Intolerable Acts against the Americans from that moment on.

The Treaty of Paris of 1763, which ended the Seven-Years war among the British, the French, and the Spanish, also put an end to the French-Indian Wars in America. As a result, the British East India Company, including the Hudson's Bay Company, became the world's No.1 colonial empire and claimed a great part of North America as its private property. Add to this the fact that the French ceded Canada and all of its claims east of the Mississippi River (most of present-day central United States), including East Louisiana. Spain ceded Florida to Britain and received West Louisiana and New Orleans from France. This established the authority of the Hudson's Bay company (The Gentlemen Adventurers) in the Rupert Territories of Canada, and the British East India Company as sole master of North America and the Seven Seas. The Gentlemen Adventurers of the British East India Company has been deep in the flank of the United States up until the nineteenth century.

The point to be made, here, is that this British operation was not a victory for King George III, but a victory for the Private British East India Company whose main nightmare was the lost potential of the American Colonies, sometimes down the road. So, when you look at the so-called "war of words" that went on between Britain and America during the period of 1763 to 1776, you have to consider that it was the "nabobs" of the East India Company who ran the British Parliament and the King, and not the other way around. This "war of words" was the prolegomena to the War of Independence.

Recall, for example, some of the misunderstandings around the Stamp Act of 1765. That Act had nothing to do with taxation of the colonies per se. Its purpose was to impose the right of the British East India Company's Parliament upon the Colonies. Its political implications were as clear to the British as they were to the colonists. This meant economic independence or servitude for American commerce and industry.

For instance, recast the memorable speech that William Pitt, Lord Chatham, made in Parliament against the Stamp Act, on January 14, 1766. In response to the Repeal of the Stamp Act by the Americans, Pitt shocked everyone by saying: I rejoice that America has resisted." Moreover, it is not surprising that in 1770, a statue of William Pitt was erected on Wall Street, commemorating his promotion of the Repeal of the Stamp Act. However, people who thought that Pitt was favorable to the Americans when he made that statement have misunderstood completely his intention. Pitt understood, at that point, that the Americans were willing to go to war in order to prevent the British East India Company's Parliament from dictating their laws. This is what Pitt agreed with: war! In the same speech, Pitt added that the power of Parliament must now be absolutely firm and *"that we may bind their trade, confine their manufactures, and exercise every power whatsoever, except that of taking their money out of their pocket without their consent."*

Thus, the British gloated, as did the chairman of the board of the British Library: *"After 1763, successive ministries determined to control the American continent more effectively, and to raise money in the colonies by a series of measures considered novel and provocative by their opponents. The Stamp Act (1765), Townshend's Duties, the setting up of a Board of Customs Commissioners (1767), and finally the Tea Act (1773), all cause resistance and riot in America and contributed to the steady accumulation of distrust and antagonism between Great*

Britain and the colonies. By the end of 1774, the two sides were set rigidly against each other." [2]

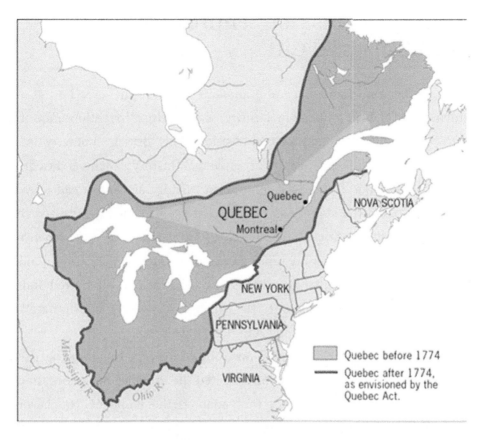

Top: The Quebec Act dramatically extended Quebec's borders in order to suffocate the colonies and block the policy of Manifest Destiny.
Below: The ownership of North America territory in 1763

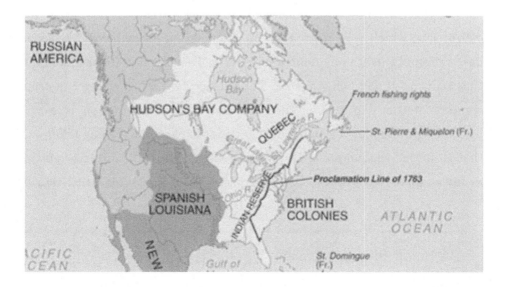

How Canadians Got "enfirouapés" into a Poisoned Gift.

From the standpoint of Canadian politics, the creation of the Province of Quebec, as a colonial entity, was a British invention under the guise of a political fallacy of composition. This British sophistry is an important piece of the puzzle of universal history, such as Friedrich Schiller understood it, because the present history of Canada can only be understood from the standpoint of this past event, which has caused that nation to become politically debilitated up until today. In 1774, when the British decided to unilaterally replace Canada by Quebec, they also intended to use Quebec as a colonial stepping-stone for attacking the United States. From that strategic standpoint, the Quebec Act was the original War Measures Act against the coming American Revolution.

In point of fact, it is quite an irony of universal history that from the moment the British had actually created the Province of Quebec, under that name, any French subject that adopted the name of "Québécois" instead of "Canadian" had been made to believe he was secure in the comfort zone of a protected French enclave, while, in fact, he was actually being short-changed by being given a British identity!

There is, in French-Canadian parlance, a curious British verbal expression, which was created during that period and which is a perfect description of this tragic moment of history. The expression translated into Québécois is: se faire enfirouaper. The Québécois think they are the proud creators of this expression. They are not. This verbal action is a very interesting metaphor which means "getting screwed," or "being taken in," that is, in the original polite British language of the 18th century: "getting in fur wrapped." It also means being protected in warm blankets. Getting enfirouaper was precisely what has happened politically and historically to the Canadian population over two hundred years ago with the Quebec Act. They got royally screwed.

In 1774, the ruling representative of British Canada, Guy Carleton, *"Captain-general and Governor in and over the Province of Quebec, and the Territories depending thereon in America"*, had the Parliament of London pass the Quebec Act, under his hand, which rendered null and void the conditions established by the 1763 Treaty of Paris, and gave to the province of Quebec its name along with its current political and legal status.

The Quebec Act of 1774, composed between May 10 and May 13, 1774, gave the French Canadians the right to practice their own religion (100 years before such a right was legitimized in England), the right to have their own judges, and apply the French Civil Code in all of their daily activities, as well as the right for the Seigneurs (Lords) to raise taxes throughout the province. Remember that the British legislated, in the same spirit, the intolerable Administration of Justice Act (May 20, 1774) against the American colonists precisely 7 days after having formulated the Quebec Act, but exactly to the opposite effect. This connection between Canadians and the Americans shows the reason why there existed no specific Canadian circumstance that warranted such a sudden change of policy and why nothing, in the annals of Canada, could be found that would explain the bounty of such a gratuitous gift as Quebec to the French colonists. Only the reference to the American Revolution can explain why the French colonial and the American colonials, each in a different way, were treated as animals. The one was enfirouapé; the other was tarred and feathered. Such is British justice.

Accompanying this generous British action in Canada, there were two infinitesimal details that remained unchanged and were considered so insignificant as not to cause the British controllers any serious concern:

the Québécois had no right to have their own government and had to swear an oath of allegiance to a British king instead of a French king. And, Bob's your uncle! However, those two insignificant details stood out like sore thumbs pointing to the significance of making the difference between man and animal. In political human terms, this infinitesimal change was the difference between the Leibnizian calculus and the Newtonian bowdlerization of the same calculus: the difference between a true change in the universe and a linear fallacy of composition faking a change. Yet, not one Canadian historian ever noticed that there existed that difference between what the Québécois were getting from the British and what the Americans were about to offer them.

Similarly, since pronouncing the name of Georges Trois appeared to be the same as saying Louis Seize, there were no objections to change allegiance as long as the Québécois colonials saw the restoration of the same French feudal rights as before 1763. Besides, the Treaty of Paris of 1763 had already dubbed Georges III king of France. This is what Carleton considered to be the essential condition to maintain the Québécois enfirouapés within their apparently fixed boundary conditions. And Carleton was convinced that such an Act, as tolerable as it could be made, would maintain the French people as contented cows. Thus, the French population was denied the right to have its own government and was given warm blankets, instead. The Québécois had discovered the British Principle of Happiness.

The Jesuit dominated Catholic Church took care of maintaining the status quo in the parishes, which was guaranteed by the bishops of Montreal and of Quebec while Carleton instituted a Governorship with a Council to rule the new province of Quebec.

Tout va bien!

The Council, located in Quebec City, had no less than 17 and no more than 23 members nominated by the Privy Council of the British Crown. In a word, the British had given the French Canadians the poisoned gift of their apparent autonomous territorial, linguistic, and religious sovereignty: the right and the ability to go along to get along.

Now, this raises the question: Did any leaders of the French community see through that charade, and did any of them stand up for the unalienable rights of man? The answer to this question is fortunately yes! That leader's name was Clement Gosselin, from La Pocatiere east of the Isle of Orleans, near Quebec City. Gosselin recruited several hundred French Canadians to the revolutionary war. The contingent of Canadian patriots and revolutionaries preferred to risk being excommunicated rather than to miss this world historical moment. The Gosselin story will be told in a forthcoming report.

According to the great grandson of this French Canadian patriot, the American historian, Henry Gosselin, his relative defied the excommunication threat by the Bishop of Quebec City, Monsignor Olivier Briand, and became the main French Canadian spy for George Washington. Gosselin added:

"Despite his pastor's warning, Clement continued to recruit other French Canadians to support the American assault on Quebec, Dec. 31, 1775. He went on to serve as a spy in Canada for General George Washington. And at Yorktown, Virginia, he was wounded while commanding an artillery unit less than 300 yards from the British in the final battle of the American Revolution. He was given 1,000 acres of land on the west bank of Lake Champlain in upstate New York by a grateful Congress. But his heart was always in the land of his birth – the Isle of Orleans in Quebec."

Clement Gosselin had estimated that if the Americans had launched their attack on Quebec City 20 days earlier, Canada would have been in their hands. *"Had the Americans arrived at Levis when Arnold hoped they would, there would have been almost nothing opposing the invaders. Quebec was a virtually defenseless city. Governor Carleton had sent two of his four regiments to defend Boston — which was precisely what the Americans wanted to prevent from happening again. And he had sent a third regiment to Montreal and Saint John. The garrison at Saint John had surrendered to General Montgomery on Nov. 2 — and the remainder of the British regulars was in Montreal, where Montgomery's forces were currently conducting a siege. The two-pronged American invasion north had left the cities of Montreal and Quebec undermanned."*[4]

The Truth behind the British Sophistry

According to official documents, the reason for the change in Canada was to create *"An Act for making more effectual Provisions for the Government of the Province of Quebec in North America, [...]"* Now, what is wrong with that? Does a population not deserve provisions for their government? Yes, of course, but what kind of provisions? What is hidden in the form of language elaborated by Carleton? Why do I consider that statement as a conscious lie? It is only by reflecting back from the American Revolution that we can make conscious the fact that the British used such "Provisions" to justify their culling of the Québécois herd in order to maintain a control over them.

Next, imagine the document stating the truth, instead. That is, bringing the pre-conscious to the level of consciousness, you might say that the reason for the change was to create: ***"An act for making more*** *effectual provisions in order to maintain "enfirouapée" the population of the Province of Quebec in North America and for preventing their joining the American Revolution, [...]"* Voila! This is the thought that was located, ontologically as Lyn would say, in a preconscious form within the previous lying statement. Of course this statement could not have been stated without subverting the entire intention of the document, but the truth emerges from it, nonetheless, as a testament to its false authenticity. Which is exactly my point. This preconscious formulation alone shows that the Quebec Act of 1774 is a historical fraud.

On the other hand, in France, a variation on the same paradox was being played by a British alliance with the Orleans French oligarchy of Philippe Egalité, the result of which made the French people captive to another British fallacy of composition that became known as the French Revolution. This was best exemplified by the neo-conservative ideology created by Martinist Synarchist and British agent, Joseph de Maistre, who succeeded in destroying the constitutional monarchy as formulated by Jean-Sylvain Bailly and Marquis de Lafayette at the Tennis Court Oath, on June 20th 1789. In other words, nowhere, since the Treaty of Paris of 1763, except for the brief moment of June 1789, did the French population succeed in rising above its littleness.

Now, the British did the same thing to the indigenous populations of Canada. They herded them into reservations out of which they have not come out to this day. Thus, it becomes clear that such an unnatural act of British subversion of Canada as a whole, and of the province of Quebec in particular, had never been instituted for the purpose of improving the condition of the French population, or for liberating them, but for the sole purpose of preventing 70,000 people of Canada from becoming the 14th colony of the United States a year before the beginning of the American War of Independence.

The Tragic Failure of the French Revolution

Despite heroic efforts by leading statesmen and scientists in 1789 led by Jean-Sylvain Bailly (top left) who initiated the Tennis Court Oath (middle top) modelled on the American Declaration of Independence, and Marquis de Lafayette (top right), the French Revolution was quickly subverted with the London-steered Jacobin movement which claimed as its banner "the revolution doesn't need scientists", as it sent Bailly, Lavoisier and countless others to the guillautine. Though republican in his heart, Lafayette's failure to break with his aristocratic conditioning caused him to flee France for his life, living in an Austrian prison for the following 5 years. Pictured below are Robespierre(left), the storming of the Batstille, and synarchist leader Joseph de Maistre

As a result of this sophistry, no French Canadian, except Clement Gosselin and his group, dared defy the new British rule and join the American revolutionaries. The Oath to King George III made it as an explicit threat against anyone who joined the American conspiracy, stating: *"I sincerely promise and swear that I will be faithful, and bear true Allegiance to His Majesty King George, and him will defend to the utmost of my Power, against all treacherous Conspiracies, and attempts whatsoever, which shall be made against His Person, Crown and Dignity; and I will do my utmost Endeavour to disclose and make known to His Majesty, His Heirs, and Successors, all Treasons, and treacherous Conspiracies, and Attempts, which I shall know to be against Him or any of Them..."*

All persons refusing to take the Oath were subject to penalties and fines, including death. In other words, not only were Gosselin and his patriots excommunicated from their Church, but they had become pariahs risking the death penalty. This was a high price to pay for not subscribing to an act, itself fallacious, that had created a synthetic entity that was to last for 244 years, with virtually no significant modifications. Today, the government of Quebec is still ruled under the unchanged "provisions" set by the fraudulent Quebec Act of 1774. Currently, the Quebec government is still controlled by the Privy Council of the British Queen, Elizabeth II.

Several American delegations, including Benjamin Franklin, Samuel Chase, Charles Carroll, and his brother John Carroll were sent to Montreal by George Washington and the Continental Congress during the American Revolution. But, not one of them was able to change the tragic situation that had been quietly established with the lie of the Quebec Act of 1774.

Treason in Canada and the Two Failed American Invasions.

The invasion of Canada was an important part of the American Revolution strategy. The idea of transforming Canada into a 14th American colony was not just a nice idea, but was a creative preconscious thought that was slowly making its way into the consciousness of even British governors during the immediate pre-revolutionary period. Canada has been a weak flank for the potential subversion of the Constitutional Republic of the United States by the British ever since 1763 and has, since then, remained an essential concern for the security of the American continent as a whole.

For example, the first American preparations for an invasion of Canada occurred in May of 1746 when, during the French and Indian War, British Governor of the Massachusetts Bay Colony, William Shirley, called on other governors and on the British Military for their assistance in this operation. It was then that the British-American Governors realized that their enemy was not only France but also Britain. Shirley did not wish to invade Canada because he wanted to liberate the French population on behalf of the American Independence. He was British-born and did not like the French, but he saw Canada as a permanent danger in the flank of America.

As a matter of fact, Shirley was quite nasty with the French Canadians. He was the commander-in-chief of the Great Expulsion that forced the deportation of more than 12,000 Acadians from Nova Scotia beginning 1755 until 1763. The Acadians had resisted the British more seriously than the Quebecois did. They did not accept the unjust conditions the British imposed on them after the Treaty of Utrecht of 1714, when France lost Newfoundland, Nova Scotia, and the Hudson Bay territories to the British.

However, as a British Governor and not as an American revolutionary, Shirley had realized the power the American colonists might have if Canada ever fell into their hands. That is why early that summer of 1746, Shirley had requested from London the authorization for his Canada expedition, explaining to the British Minister of War, the Duke of Newcastle, that the governors of the colonies were willing to raise troops and take Canada from the French. These were all American Red Coats under British command. The Duke accepted the proposal. As reported by historian Graham Lowry: *"Massachusetts voted to raise 3,500 men; Connecticut 1,000; New Hampshire, 500; and Rhode Island 300. The Duke of New Castle, now chief minister, had promised to send a squadron with eight battalions of British regulars, to join the New England troops at Louisburg, for an attack up the St. Lawrence against Quebec. Like the expedition of 1711, the plan called for a simultaneous assault by land on Montreal, from northern New York. For this second army, New York raised 1,600 men. New Jersey 500, and Maryland 300. Virginia managed 100 more, despite the decided lack of enthusiasm on the part of Governor Gooch. Gooch's attitude did not bode well, since the ministry had designated him Major general, to command the American attack on Montreal."*[5]

By July, the news had reached the Americans that the British contingent was not coming from Britain and the American invasion of Canada fell apart. Through British intelligence machinations, the French got wind of the invasion plan and sent 3,150 veteran troops to retake Louisburg immediately, thus, obliterating any American attempt at taking Canada. Meanwhile, the British had cancelled their own military expedition and the Duke of Newcastle waited another four months before ordering the American regiments to disband before winter came. The British obviously never intended to take Canada for the benefit of the Americans. This treasonous alliance of 1746 between the French and the British oligarchies was still a living memory when, in 1775, a second American attempt was made to take Canada, this time, by soliciting its people in joining the American Revolution.

On September 16, 1775, Major General Richard Montgomery was ordered by General Washington to march north from Fort Ticonderoga with 1,700 troops in an attempt to capture Montreal. According to American historian Michael P. Gabriel, who wrote the monography *Major General Richard Montgomery: the Making of an American Hero*, Montgomery was born of Irish gentry with an inbred "noblesse oblige" military outlook. But, however determined Montgomery might have been, there was already a sabotage operation underway. There was another operation that beat him to the punch by attacking Montreal before he got there.

When On September 25, out of his own initiative, Ethan Allen and his renegade Green Mountain Boys attacked Montreal and lost against Carleton, Allen was made prisoner of war. What happened to Allen's troops remains uncertain, but Allen, himself, was reportedly later shipped to prison in England and returned to America in exchange for a British prisoner two years later. On November 13, Montgomery took Montreal without difficulty, but was unable to capture the Governor of Canada, General Guy Carleton, who made his escape to Quebec City with his British troops. The reason for the escape of Carleton is obscure and remains a mystery.

In the book *The War of the American Revolution*, Robert Coakley described the invasion of Canada in the following way:

"Montgomery, advancing along the route via Lake George, Lake Champlain, and the Richelieu River, was seriously delayed by the British fort at St. Johns but managed to capture Montreal on November 13. Arnold meanwhile had

arrived opposite Quebec on November 8, after one of the most rugged marches in history. One part of his force had turned back and others were lost by starvation, sickness, drowning, and desertion. Only 600 men crossed the St. Lawrence on November 13, and in imitation of Wolfe scaled the cliffs and encamped on the Plains of Abraham. It was a magnificent feat, but the force was too small to prevail even against the scattered Canadian militia and British Regulars who, unlike Montcalm, shut themselves up in the city and refused battle in the open. Arnold's men were finally forced to withdraw to Point aux Trembles, where they were joined by Montgomery with all the men he could spare from the defense of Montreal a total of 300. Nowhere did the Canadians show much inclination to rally to the American cause; the French habitants remained indifferent, and the small British population gave its loyalty to the governor general. With the enlistments of about half their men expiring by the New Year, Arnold and Montgomery undertook a desperate assault on the city during the night of December 30 in the middle of a raging blizzard. The Americans were outnumbered by the defenders, and the attack was a failure. Montgomery was killed and Arnold wounded." [6]*

What is not clear is how Montgomery managed to take Montreal on November 13 after Ethan Allen had failed in his premature attack on September 25. The idea was to take Canada before the winter sets in, however, by December, Montgomery had not yet secured his victory and had to launch a second expedition with Colonel Benedict Arnold in Quebec City. But Arnold had been in the sight of the enemy in Quebec since November. What was he waiting for? Several things remain to be clarified with respect to this attack of the Citadel of Quebec City in the middle of a raging snowstorm. Was that a suicidal mission, some sort of Wintry Charge of the Light Brigade? Why would the Americans attack under such incredible odds? The true roles of Carleton, Allen, and Arnold remain to be further investigated. Michael Gabriel made the following revealing statement about the tragic end of Richard Montgomery.

"*Spending fifteen years in the British army, Montgomery saw extensive action during the French and Indian War at such places as Fortress Louisburg and Fort Ticonderoga. However, he was heavily influenced by opposition ideology, grew disillusioned with Britain, and permanently immigrated to America in 1772, where he became a gentleman farmer. Marrying into a powerful New York Livingston family, Montgomery reluctantly embraced the American cause as the imperial crisis deepened, as he still felt ties for Britain and his old regiment. He served first as a delegate in the New York Provincial Congress and then as a brigadier general in the Continental Army. On the night of December 30-31, 1775, faced with expiring enlistments, Montgomery launched a disastrous assault on Quebec, which cost him his life and effectively ended the American bid to seize Canada.*"[7]

After Montgomery had been killed, it remained unclear as to what happened to the remaining American troops. How did they spend the rest of the rough Canadian winter? Were they in hiding? Were they trapped and forced to surrender? Did Benedict Arnold make a deal with Carleton? Montgomery had only brought to Quebec City 300 men from an initial 1,700 troops and Arnold only had 650 men left out of an initial army of 1,150 men. That is a lot of people to lose along the way. One report indicated that 100 Americans had fallen in the attack on Quebec, and 400 were made prisoners.

Captain Daniel Morgan, who became the Commanding officer after the wounding of Arnold, was made prisoner along with 372 men captured. Morgan was released in January 1777. However, another story claims that the remains of the American army managed to stay in the surroundings of Quebec City for the rest of the winter (during four entire months) before withdrawing to Lake Champlain by spring of 1776. Another report says that

Carleton drove the Americans past Trois Rivieres in June of 1776. There are a lot of conflicting accounts. What kind of agreement was made between Carleton and Arnold to assure the safe conduit of the last 400 American troops back to the American colonies? It is well known that Carleton did not launch a counterattack against Arnold until October of 1776, defeating him at the Battle of Valcourt Island on Lake Champlain. It was then that Arnold retreated to Fort Ticonderoga, which had been the initial staging ground for the Canadian invasion in the first place.

I raise all of these questions because the treasons of Ethan Allen and of Benedict Arnold warrant such an investigation. It is not an accident that Benedict Arnold would begin his military career by first teaming up with Ethan Allen at Fort Ticonderoga, which is the place where the invasion of Canada took its roots. Moreover, this second invasion of Canada turned out to be a major defeat for the Americans, yet the efforts of Arnold and Allen have been played by historians as being helpful in delaying a full-scale British offensive from the north until 1777. Was that really the case? Did Benedict Arnold begin his treason as early as 1775 in Ticonderoga or Quebec City? What was the true relationship between the two traitors, Allen and Arnold? Here are a few leads that I think should be pursued.

Ethan Allen was the leader of a sort of vigilante group called the Green Mountain Boys. On May 10, 1775, five months before initiating the invasion of Canada, Ethan Allen and his renegade type of Green Mountain Boys were getting ready to capture Fort Ticonderoga on Lake Champlain when, "out of the blue," Benedict Arnold showed up and presented himself to Allen with "official papers" giving him command of the same expedition. Reportedly, after a first moment of friction between the two, Allen and Arnold finally agreed to work together.

They took Fort Ticonderoga by complete surprise in the middle of the night and captured its 50 or so soldiers without firing a shot. The

British fort commander was unaware that the historical shot had been fired at Concord. Both Allen and Arnold went on to capture, together again, fortifications at Crown Point, Fort St John, on the Richelieu River, and Fort Ann on Isle La Motte. This should have cleared the way for Montgomery. So, why was he delayed at fort St. John before taking Montreal in November?

Both Allen and Arnold were malcontent and ambitious military men who became traitors to the Revolution. Arnold was not a man of principle and he wanted to get recognition from the Continental Congress. As a result of his discontent, in his capacity of Commandant of West Point, Arnold wrote the following letter to British General Henry Clinton: *"If I point out a plan of cooperation, Sir Henry shall be the master of West Point. 20 000-pound sterling will be a cheap purchase for an object of so much importance. I expect a full and explicit answer."* [8] That treasonous statement was found in the possession of Arnold's friend, the aide de camp of General Clinton, Major John Andre, on the day he was arrested near West Point, September 21, 1780. That same night, Benedict Arnold made his escape from West Point to join the British ship, The Vulture, on the Hudson River.

On the other hand, in 1778, Ethan Allen was appointed general in the Army of Vermont, when he petitioned the Continental Congress on behalf of the statehood of Vermont against the claims of New Hampshire and New York states. After the Congress rejected Allen's proposal, he turned to the enemy side and began negotiating for establishing of Vermont as a British appendage to the Province of Quebec with the same Governor, Guy Carleton, who had made him a prisoner of war in Montreal three years earlier. At that point, the Continental Congress charged Allen with treason but, for reasons that remain to be clarified, the charge was never carried through.

What is interesting, in all of this, is that every time the Americans attempt to take over Canada, the operations are always fraught with treason.

The Death of General Wolf by Benjamin West. 1770. The British victory on the Plains of Abraham, on September 13, 1756, was the imperial axiomatic moment of the Seven Years War that set the strategic conditions for the American Revolution twenty years later.

left to right: Sir Guy Carleton, Benedict Arnold and Major Andre

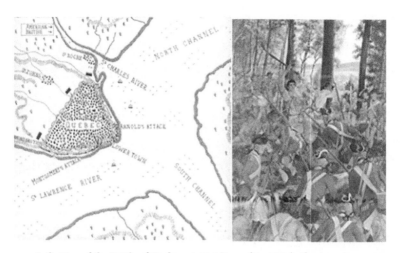

Left: Map of the Battle of Quebec on 31st December 1775 in the American Revolutionary War (map by John Fawkes) Right: Fighting at Montreal in September 1775

French Canadians fighting Americans in Quebec City 1775

Repeal the Quebec Act of 1774 and Bring the Principle of Westphalia to Canada

If this subversive Quebec Act of 1774, has had the historical effect of isolating the French population of Quebec from the rest of Canada, it also had also wronged the rest of Canadians, proportionately, to the effect of making them dependent on an artificial form of religious, political, and linguistic exceptionalism. This explains why Canada has been reduced to a state of tragic political impotence for such a long period of time. The tragedy is that Canada has been established on a false protectionist pretense and nothing but the repudiation of this historical fallacy can begin repairing the wrong that has been done to the people of that nation for over two centuries.

Canada will never be able to restore its dignity as a sovereign nation-state until the Act of Quebec is repealed, and the status of sovereign dignity of equal partnership between all of the minorities of Canada, including its autochthonous peoples, is fully restored in accordance with the truthful community of principle common to sovereign nation-states. It is the truth of universal history that demands that this act of injustice be forcefully corrected, now, before the court of history and for the sake of future generations.

The time has come for a bold and generous action that will bring the Mazarin and Colbert spirit of the Peace of Westphalia to Canada. It is time that the principle of concern for other peoples should take precedence over one's own personal interest. It is time to reunite all of the peoples of the province of Quebec properly within a sovereign constitutional federation of Canada based on the principle of the Advantage of the Other. It is time for all of the minorities of Canada, as one indivisible sovereign nation-state, to break with that fallacy of territorial reservation known as the Quebec Act of 1774, and to sever ties with the British oligarchy that invented such a fallacy of composition, which led to 244 years of ruinous effects. This doesn't mean to sever all ties with England, Ireland and Scotland; this means that the time has come for Canada to break openly with the oligarchical principle of the British Empire. Once this is done, Canada can participate honestly and truthfully in the community of sovereign nations-states for the common aims of mankind.

The swearing of the Oath of Ratification of the Treaty of Munster that ended the 80-year war (1568-1648) between Spain and the Netherlands, on 15 May 1648, by Gerard Terborch. In attendance were all of the negotiators of the Peace of Westphalia, which was signed simultaneously in Munster for the Catholics and in Osnabruck for the Protestants five months later, on 24 October 1648. The Peace of Westphalia created the basis for the modern sovereign nation-state.

Below: Cardinal Jules Mazarin (right) who led in organizing the Peace and his protege Jean-Baptistte Colbert (left) who carried this policy into North America. Colbert's ideas directly influenced many founding fathers of America as they formulated the legal basis for the new republic.

CHAPTER II - GO WEST YOUNG MAN! THE IMPORTANCE OF MANIFEST DESTINY FOR CANADIAN HISTORY

I n 1776, at the time when in the American colonies, the greatest liberation movement in all of history was asserting itself, as the *"Beacon of Hope and the Temple of Liberty"* for all of mankind, a wall of British oligarchical lies, known as the Quebec Act of 1774, was erected around a *"neighboring Province"* in order to prevent the United States from being born. For the American Continental Congress, the Quebec Act became the most important reason for pushing the 13 colonies of America to unite and to *"dissolve their political bands"* with Britain on July 4, 1776.

The irony of this Quebec Act is that it was not designed for improving the lives of Canadians, but for the purpose of destroying Americans and their constitutional principles. This Intolerable Act, as it was called in America, was concocted by the British East India Company, otherwise known as the Lords of Trade and Plantations, for extending invasively the territorial boundaries of the Province of Quebec deep inside of the American territory, south to the Ohio River and West to the Mississippi River, by means of the Gentleman Adventurer's Hudson's Bay Company, in order to prevent the Americans from reaching westward toward the Pacific Ocean, thereby, putting an end to the unique experiment of American exceptionalism, that is, George Washington's *Manifest Destiny*. From that strategic standpoint, both North and South America were to be secured and isolated from the infection of British oligarchism that had taken root in Canada. It was within the context of that exceptional moment of history that the Quebec Act was also meant to prevent the French Canadians from joining the American Revolution. Moreover, this infectious disease known as the Quebec Act was to hang like a Damocles' sword over the Americas from that day forward.

Since the Quebec Act is still, to this day, the founding document that established British Canada as a colony, the following thoughts are therefore aimed at provoking public discussion that will help define political guidelines for taking appropriate actions in changing this continuously intolerable and fraudulent state of affairs inside of Canada, and to see how that nation-state can become a fruitful participant in the Grand Design of the LaRouche Bering Strait tunnel proposal linking up the Americas with Eurasia.

If 1776 reflected a great moment of history that was missed by a little people in Canada, let it be understood that the current opportunity of the Grand Design of the LaRouche-Gilpin Bering Strait Tunnel proposal, today, is a similar moment of history. So, the question is: *will the Canadian people seize the opportunity of joining this second American Revolution?*

Here, however, a note of caution is required. These questions are not aimed at raising a public debate over the Constitutionality of Canada at this time. It would have been better to initiate that dialogue, a few years ago, when the Vancouver proposal for a constitutional consensus amendment formula was introduced. But it is too late for that now. However, there is a preliminary step which can be taken before a full debate over the Constitutional reform of Canada may be undertaken. The focus for raising these questions must be the mission of planetary self-development for the next fifty years, along the lines of the Eurasian Landbridge and the Bering Strait. This requires absolutely that Canadian citizens and Canadian political leaders resolve in their own minds the crucial anomalies posed by the Quebec Act. Without solving these fundamental questions, there is no chance that Canada could appropriately tackle the challenge of the next fifty years and more, in collaboration with the four primary powers, namely, the United States, Russia, China, and India. Therefore the time has come to get rid of the fallacious British oligarchical thinking that has been preventing the nation of Canada and the rest of the world from developing.

America's Manifest Destiny.

In the retrospective search for attempting to explain the causes for the deeply rooted discontent between the English and French in Canada, invariably, one has to come to grips with the nature of the Quebec Act of 1774 that created the modern form of Canada in the first place. So, investigating the historical specificities that derived from this legislation is the prerequisite historical work that can help explain what caused the present state of political and cultural crisis in Canada. This work will also help us discover the alternate policies that will restore Canada as a more truthful sovereign nation-state for future generations. Therefore, the first and most important aspect to be considered lies in the fact that this intolerable Quebec Act did not succeed in destroying Americans but has been destroying Canadians for over 200 years. In other words, to this day,

The blossoming of a new nation

Above: Scene at the Signing of the Constitution of the United States
by Howard Chandler Christy. 1940

Below: "Westward Ho!" by Emmanuel Leutze

this founding legislation has not been serving its intended purpose. This is not a matter to be taken lightly and with fleeting discussions; this is a matter of life and death for a people and its posterity.

The truth of this matter is so crucial that it was deemed necessary to be included explicitly in the American Declaration of Independence itself. The signers of the Declaration denounced this Quebec Act:

"For abolishing the free System of English Laws in a neighbouring Province, establishing therein an Arbitrary government, and enlarging its Boundaries as to render it at once an example and fit instrument for introducing the same absolute rule into these Colonies."

There are two points to be considered here. One is with regard to Americans and the other is with respect to Canadians.

To Americans, the Quebec Act was considered to be the most dangerous of all five Intolerable Acts legislated by the British Parliament between 1763 and 1774. The Quebec Act created, in North America, the precedent that actually banned the idea of self-government and erected a barrier against the George Washington project of *Manifest destiny*, that is, the project for the development of western territories all the way to the Pacific Ocean. This *Manifest Destiny* idea was precisely the original root-idea that gave birth to Lyndon LaRouche's Bering Strait project, linking the entire world with anti-oligarchical republics around the principle of basic human rights and self-development of constitutionally sovereign nation-states and grounded in the principle of the benefit of the other of the Peace of Westphalia.

Contrary to popular belief, the idea of *Manifest Destiny* actually originated in ancient Greece, with Solon of Athens. It was later restored with the Renaissance of Nicholas of Cusa and was defined in America by the founder of New England, John Winthrop. The founding father who most embodied the idea of *Manifest Destiny* was Silas Deane. However, the idea became the official American policy doctrine under John Quincy

Adams and was established as the basis for a community of principle in his Monroe Doctrine. This policy is always standing today and must pursued with renewed vigor. [1]

The term "destiny" attached to this policy was coined originally by John Quincy Adams in a letter written from Russia to his father John Adams, and in which he stated:

"The whole continent of North America appears to be destined by Divine providence to be peopled by one nation, speaking one language, professing one general system of religious and political principles, and accustomed to one general tenor of social usages and customs. For the common happiness of them all, for their peace and prosperity, I believe it indispensable that they should be associated in one federal Union."[2]

The idea was meant to cut off the newly created republic from the poison of oligarchism coming from the East and to push the development of American republicanism westward. Bring civilization to the West. *"The struggle was always—colonize westward"*, noted Lyndon LaRouche. *"Bring the best people from Europe, the best common people who believed in this idea; bring them to this land, develop this land, move westward, open the way to the west, keep moving westward."[3]*

This is why, in their *Declarations and Resolves of Oct. 14, 1774*, the American Continental Congress of Philadelphia recognized that the Quebec Act was a direct assault against the idea of Manifest Destiny. They identified the Quebec Act as being *"unjust, and cruel, as well as unconstitutional, and most dangerous and destructive of American rights."* I will recall, here, only a few of the most vocal American leaders who denounced the Quebec Act for the fallacy of composition that it is and for the danger it represented against the American progress of civilization westward.

On October 21, 1774, John Jay, the first Chief Justice from New York, drafted a letter to the People of Great Britain, in which he denounced the Quebec Act as follows:

"In the session of parliament last mentioned, an act was passed, for changing the government of Quebec, by which act the Roman Catholic religion, instead of being tolerated, as stipulated by the treaty of peace, is established; and the people there deprived of a right to an assembly, trials by jury and the English laws in civil cases abolished, and instead thereof, the French laws established, in direct violation of his Majesty's promise by his royal proclamation, under the faith of which many English subjects settled in that province: and the limits of that province are extended so as to comprehend those vast regions, that lie adjoining to the northerly and westerly boundaries of these colonies."[4]

On the same day (October 21, 1774), Patrick Henry of Virginia drafted the following address to the king:

"Judge Royal Sir what must be our feelings when we see our fellow subjects of that Town & Colony suffering a Severity of punishment of which the British History gives no Example, & the Annals of Tyranny can scarcely equal? And when we see in the Fate of this our sister Colony that which awaits us, we are filled with the most terrible apprehensions–Apprehensions which are heightened & increased almost to Despair, when we turn our Attention to the Quebec Act."

It was Silas "Ticonderoga" Deane, Chairman of the Committee on Safety for the colony of Connecticut, who sounded the alarm about the explicit danger to *Manifest Destiny*, by sending a letter to Samuel Adams, Chairman of the same committee for Massachusetts, warning him of the dangers respecting western territories. Deane called for immediate migration of large numbers of Europeans (up to a million settlers) to stake their claims in these territories. He considered that *"This, or some such plan, will most effectually defeat the design of the Quebec Bill, which if not broke thro' & defeated in some shape or other, will be the most fatally mischievous to the British*

Colonies of any Bill ever framed by the Ministry, or that may possibly ever enter into their Hearts To conceive of." In fact, the Quebec Act had stripped Massachusetts, Connecticut, Pennsylvania, and Virginia of their lawful claims to western lands. Like Silas Deane, the Virginian, Richard Henry Lee, considered the Quebec Act as the "*worst grievance*" of all intolerable acts against America.

On November 13, 1774, Silas Dean explained why the Quebec Act represented such a great danger to the grand design of ***Manifest Destiny***.

"*The extending & fixing Settlements of Protestants Westward will not only bring about this wished-for event, but will be in future Days Our greatest Strength & Security. Another Tier as I may say of Colonies settled back of us will be, an inexhaustible resource to Us, &c render Us humanely speaking invincible though the united Powers of the whole World should attack Us. Look at a Map, & see, the situation of the Countries between 40.° & 45.° through the Continent. This is the New England Inheritance, as fairly secured for them, by their Ancestors, as any one Acre they now possess, and once well settled with our People, & their descendants, will give Law, not to North & South America alone, but to the World if they please.*

"*This will, & must be the most independent Country on the Globe, inland Seas or Lakes, and Rivers extending quite across the Continent in those parallels, and the Western extremity lands Us at the very Door, of the Treasures of the East, and The South. If the Contemplation of these future events give Us pleasure every effort of Ours to ripen them if successful, in degree realizes them. This can hardly be called the pleasure of the imagination only, but rather the pleasure of anticipating great, & important realities, & such as are hastening on, &in the arrival of which, the happiness of Mankind is most deeply interested.*" [6]

Above left to right: Patrick Henry and a young John Quincy Adams (by John Copley)

Below (left to right): Silas Deane (by William Johnston) and

John Jay (by Gilbert Stewart) - all photos from Wiki Commons

The American Congress Invitation to French-Canadians

For the benefit of Canadians, however, the most important American intervention against the Quebec Act came on October 26, 1774, from Richard Henry Lee, a Senator from Virginia, who drafted for the Continental Congress a 12-page letter *To the Inhabitants of Quebec*, calling on the French-Canadians to repudiate the Act and join the American Revolution.

"[...] The injuries of Boston have roused and associated every colony, from Nova-Scotia to Georgia. Your province is the only link wanting, to complete the bright and strong chain of union. Nature has joined your country to theirs. Do you join your political interests? For their own sakes, they never will desert or betray you. Be assured, that the happiness of a people inevitably depends on their liberty, and their spirit to assert it. The value and extent of the advantages tendered to you are immense. Heaven grant you may not discover them to be blessings after they have bid you an eternal adieu."

"We are too well acquainted with the liberality of sentiment distinguishing your nation to imagine, that difference of religion will prejudice you against a hearty amity with us. You know that the transcendent nature of freedom elevates those who unite in her cause above all such low-minded infirmities. The Swiss Cantons furnish a memorable proof of this truth. Their union is composed of Roman Catholic and Protestant States, living in the utmost concord and peace with one another and thereby enabled, ever since they bravely vindicated their freedom, to defy and defeat every tyrant that has invaded them. [...]"

After describing to the French-Canadians the American *"invaluable rights"*; 1) the right to share in one's own government; 2) the right to a trial by jury; 3) the right of liberty of the person with a writ of Habeas Corpus; 4) the right of holding lands by the tenure of easy rent; and 5) the right of freedom of the press, the letter made an amazing critique of the Quebec Act by identifying its shortcomings, point by point.

"These are the invaluable rights that form a considerable part of our mild system of government; that, sending its equitable energy through all ranks and classes of men, defends the poor from the rich, the weak from the powerful, the industrious from the rapacious, the peaceable from the violent, the tenants from the lords, and all from their superiors.

"These are the rights without which a people cannot be free and happy, and under the protecting and encouraging influence of which these colonies have hitherto so amazingly flourished and increased.

"These are the rights a profligate Ministry are now striving by force of arms to ravish from us, and which we are with one mind resolved never to resign but with our lives.

"These are the rights you are entitled to and ought at this moment in perfection to exercise. And what is offered to you by the late Act of Parliament in their place? Liberty of conscience in your religion? No. God gave it to you; and the temporal powers with which you have been and are connected, firmly stipulated for your enjoyment of it. If laws, divine and human, could secure it against the despotic caprices of wicked men, it was secured before.

"Are the French laws in civil cases restored? It seems so. But observe the cautious kindness of the Ministers, who pretend to be your benefactors. The words of the statute are-that those "laws shall be the rule, until they shall be varied or altered by any ordinances of the Governor and Council." Is the "certainty and lenity of the criminal law of England, and its benefits and advantages," commended in the said statute, and said to "have been sensibly felt by you," secured to you and your descendants? No. They too are subjected to arbitrary "alterations" by the Governor and Council; and a power is expressly reserved of

appointing "such courts of criminal, civil and ecclesiastical jurisdiction, as shall be thought proper." Such is the precarious tenure of mere will by which you hold your lives and religion.

"The Crown and its Ministers are empowered, as far as they could be by Parliament, to establish even the Inquisition itself among you. Have you an Assembly composed of worthy men, elected by yourselves and in whom you can confide, to make laws for you, to watch over your welfare, and to direct in what quantity and in what manner your money shall be taken from you? No. The Power of making laws for you is lodged in the governor and council, all of them dependent upon and removable at the pleasure of a Minister.

"Besides, another late statute, made without your consent, has subjected you to the impositions of Excise, the horror of all free states, thus wresting your property from you by the most odious of taxes and laying open to insolent tax-gatherers, houses, the scenes of domestic peace and comfort and called the castles of English subjects in the books of their law. And in the very act for altering your government, and intended to flatter you, you are not authorized to "assess levy, or apply any rates and taxes, but for the inferior purposes of making roads, and erecting and repairing public buildings, or for other local conveniences, within your respective towns and districts." Why this degrading distinction? Ought not the property, honestly acquired by Canadians, to be held as sacred as that of Englishmen? Have not Canadians sense enough to attend to any other public affairs than gathering stones from one place and piling them up in another?

"Unhappy people! Who are not only injured, but insulted. Nay more! With such a superlative contempt of your understanding and spirit has an insolent Ministry presumed to think of you, our respectable fellow-subjects, according to the information we have received, as firmly to persuade themselves that your gratitude for the injuries and insults they have recently offered to you will engage you to take up arms and render yourselves the ridicule and detestation of the world, by becoming tools in their hands, to assist them in taking that freedom from us which they have treacherously denied to you; the unavoidable consequence of which attempt, if successful, would be the extinction of all hopes of you or your posterity being ever restored to freedom. For idiocy itself cannot believe that, when their drudgery is performed, they will treat you with less cruelty than they have us who are of the same blood with themselves.

"What would your countryman, the immortal Montesquieu, have said to such a plan of domination as has been framed for you? Hear his words, with an intenseness of thought suited to the importance of the subject.— 'In a free state, every man, who is supposed a free agent, ought to be concerned in his own government: Therefore the legislative should reside in the whole body of the people, or their representatives.'—The political liberty of the subject is a tranquility of mind, arising from the opinion each person has of his safety. In order to have this liberty, it is requisite the government be so constituted, as that one man need not be afraid of another. When the power of making laws, and the power of executing them, are united in the same person, or in the same body of Magistrates, there can be no liberty; because apprehensions may arise, lest the same Monarch or Senate, should enact tyrannical laws, to execute them in a tyrannical manner.

"The power of judging should be exercised by persons taken from the body of the people, at certain times of the year, and pursuant to a form and manner prescribed by law. There is no liberty, if the power of judging be not separated from the legislative and executive powers." [...]

"We do not ask you, by this address, to commence acts of hostility against the government of our common Sovereign. We only invite you to consult your own glory and welfare, and not to suffer yourselves to be inveigled or intimidated by infamous ministers so far as to become the instruments of their cruelty and despotism, but to unite with us in one social compact, formed on the generous principles of equal liberty and cemented by such an exchange of beneficial and endearing offices as to render it perpetual. In order to complete this highly *desirable union, we submit it to your consideration whether it may not be expedient for you to meet together in your several towns and districts and elect Deputies, who afterwards meeting in a provincial Congress, may chose Delegates to represent your province in the continental Congress to be held at Philadelphia on the tenth day of May, 1775."[7]*

The point to be made here, for Canadians, is that the entire sequence of historical events, which have shaped the national character of Canada for the last 244 years, including most prominently the conflicts between the French and English parts of its population, have been caused by the fallacy of this fraudulent Act of Quebec as explained by the members of the American Continental Congress. This means that the very history of Canada cannot be understood without explicit reference to the American Declaration of Independence prepared and established by such a Continental Congress and without investigating its historical specificity with respect to Canada. This must be done simply because the *Arbitrary government*, created by that Quebec Act, had been designed, in reality, under the guise of flattery. How can the people of a nation live under such false pretense of its founding moment and continue living the same lie after two centuries, year in and year out, without ever looking for ways and means to properly correct that long standing mistake?

Now, unless the Americans were wrong in their declarative judgment of 1776, this also means that, for Canadians, the Act of Quebec must also be adjudicated as intolerable to themselves, as against their own self-interest, and that the matter must be dealt with, consequently, in light of the very same principles that the British had trampled on almost three hundred years ago. Indeed, if the signers of the American Declaration of Independence saw fit to explicitly identify that neighbouring "Arbitrary government," as evil and despicable to human freedom, its correction must therefore be viewed by Canadians from the vantage point of the very same principles of *life, liberty, and the pursuit of happiness*, that such an Act had been aimed at eradicating also in Canada during the last two centuries.

So, in the spirit of the American *Manifest Destiny*, the time has come for Canadians to break with the chains of oligarchism within your own minds. Let's get to work! Go West young man!

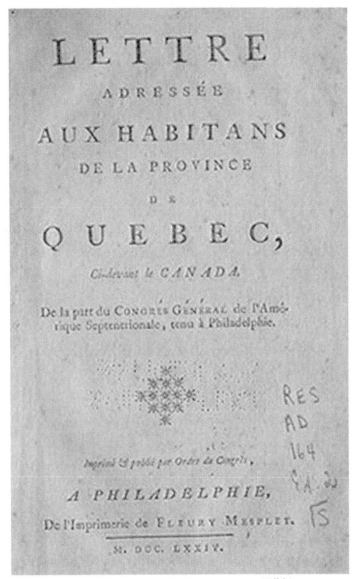

The cover of the 1774 letter issued by the Continental Congress to the Inhabitants of Quebec. Printed by Fleury Mesplet (founder of the Montreal Gazette)

CHAPTER III - CLEMENT GOSSELIN: CANADIAN PATRIOT AND AMERICAN REVOLUTIONARY

For centuries, British imperialists have developed, through their Intelligence Services, the art of convincing people into forging and wearing their own mental chains, by making them accept to go along to get along. This is how the Québec Act of 1774 was used to prevent the French-Canadian population from joining the American Revolution and kept them fenced into a pseudo-national identity.

The greatest weakness the British exploited against the French people of Canada was their lack of education. In fact, one of the most striking aspect of the historically specific 1774 period in North America was that, by that time, several generations of Americans had already been in control of their own colonial governments, had already developed extensive economic capabilities, and had been engaged in international commerce for over a century.

During the same period in Canada, however, where the population was about the same as in the American colonies, 65,000 French-Canadians had not yet acquired the cultural and political maturity to develop a nation-state and had no economics or trade system to speak of, except the fur trade between Indians and the *coureurs des bois* run by the Jesuits and the British. There were no printing presses, no Canadian books or newspapers, and no universities.

While the Americans had already founded Massachusetts' Harvard University, in 1636, and had already four universities by 1740, the very first book printed in Canada was the *Catechism*, published in 1765 by the top Catholic ally of British Governor Guy Carleton, Bishop Olivier Briand of Québec City. No other books had come out of the printing press in Canada before that date. The first French-Canadian University was Québec City's Laval University created for the curious pleasure of Queen Victoria, in 1852, over three quarters of a century after the American Revolution!

Is it any great surprise, therefore, that the majority of the French-Canadian people would have some difficulty in understanding what the American call for freedom was really all about, in 1774? Most of them did not even know how to read or write. At best, some of them joined the Americans out of rage, because they hated what the British had done to their homes and families during and after the conquest of 1759. However, in spite of such aversive cultural backwardness and regardless of British ideological manipulation, a revolutionary patriot like Clément Gosselin emerged above this bestialized containment and organized a movement in Canada to participate in the independence of America.

Wiki Commons   Wiki Commons

Top left and right: Clement Gosselin and George Washington (by Rembrandt Peale)

Bottom: Map of British Territories after the 1774 Quebec Act by William Fadden

(New York Public Library)

A Proud Moment for All Canadians

Most people, in the United States and Canada, have never heard of Clément Gosselin and don't know that, by the time of the Declaration of Independence of July 4, 1776, he had already recruited several hundred French-Canadians to join the American Revolutionary War. After pondering on the Continental Congress letter *To the Inhabitants of the Province of Québec*, Gosselin decided to participate in major battles against the British in Québec City, on Lake Champlain in New York, and in several other American colonies until he and his recruits, ultimately, joined the French and American troops in the final battle of Yorktown, Virginia, October 19, 1781, forcing the capitulation of the British and securing liberty and independence for the American people.

In this present report, my purpose is three-fold: one is to establish the historical context in which the American strategy of *Manifest Destiny* came to be deployed; two is to give a clinical account of the British Intelligence operation against Clément Gosselin and his French-Canadian recruits; and three is to have the reader walk through the angst and pains of what must have been required for a French-Canadian leader of that period to accomplish such a revolutionary change, in himself and in his people.

Clément Gosselin, son of Gabriel Gosselin and Genevieve Crépeaux, was born June 12, 1747, in the Sainte Famille parish on the Isle of Orleans, east of Québec City. Like his father, Clément became a carpenter by profession. He was living in La Pocatiere, Québec, when he joined the Americans with about 200 other French-Canadians, in the ill-fated attack of General Richard Montgomery against Québec City, on December 31, 1775. The young 28 year-old Clément, was not shaken by this American defeat, and rapidly became the main recruiter of French-Canadian troops for

Colonel Benedict Arnold's returning expedition. He later joined Moses Hazen's Second Canadian Regiment with the rank of Captain. Captain Clément Gosselin was, also, subsequently chosen to become George Washington's personal Canadian military intelligence informant. Two letters of Gosselin found in George Washington's collected papers attest to that.

One of the most fascinating aspects of this little known story of Clément Gosselin is the sublime courage with which he and several hundreds of other French-Canadians he recruited, fought successfully against the barrage of British psychological warfare, systematically waged against them, and their families. Gosselin was personally singled out and targeted by British intelligence as the leader of the group. Ultimately, these exceptional French-Canadians burnt their bridges with the British regime, abandoned all of their properties behind them, broke ranks with the consensus of public opinion represented by their relatives, parish priests, and Bishops, and even defied excommunication pronouncements against them by the highest Prelate of Canada, in order to liberate themselves from the bestial conditions the British rulers had imposed on Canada and America during the eighteenth century.

The story of Captain Gosselin is not about a hero of some romantic adventure, or about a rebel reacting against authority. This is the story, simple and beautiful, of a revolutionary struggle between a man's quest to free his people and a monstrous cabal of religious and political alliance that kept the minds of French-Canadians in shackles like cattle in a paddock during the entire course of the American Revolutionary War. This is the story of what Benjamin Franklin had identified as the central anomaly of the American Revolution itself, and that every American colonist also had to resolve for himself or herself, that is:

"Those who would sacrifice liberty for security deserve neither."

It was precisely the paradox of *security and liberty* that Clément Gosselin had to resolve by developing in himself and in others, the higher powers of understanding the universal physical principle that was embodied in the very fabric of the American movement for independence. The question was: how do you break the mental chains of a self-imposed need to secure one's life based on the social security consensus of mass public opinion?

On the one hand, as Frederick Schiller showed in the case of the French Revolution, history often presents itself as a tragedy appearing in the form of a cultural flaw in which *"a great moment of history meets a little people."* The history of the creation of the Province of Québec by the British Québec Act of 1774, had provided the boundary conditions for such a tragedy to emerge, but the cause of that calamity did not come from the imposition of the Québec Act, as such. The tragedy was caused by the collective acceptance of the apparent security that this Act provided, fallaciously, to the French-Canadian population. The British occupants of Québec hypocritically protected the French-Canadians against the American Revolution and provided them with what the French-Canadians thought was going to secure their well-being as a nation. It was a total delusion. The population got itself *enfirwapée,* as they put it in the Québecois Franglish language of the period: they got themselves completely wrapped up in fur, that is to say, *fourrés* (screwed) by their need for security.

On the other hand, what the French-Canadians who decided to fight back against the British realized was that their freedom was not going to be handed to them on a platter by the invading Americans and that they would have to fight for their own political freedom by breaking with their own mental-chains. They refused to follow the great majority who were not willing to sacrifice the little they had for something they had little or not understanding of. Therefore, only a few hundreds decided to make the decisive axiomatic change. Regardless, given the ratio of those few to the total population, this extraordinary transformation was a unique and outstanding accomplishment, never to be replicated again.

Thus, this lesson in universal history takes us back to a *punctum saliens*, a strategic turning point that led to the British occupation of Canada and to an attempted sabotage of America's *Manifest Destiny* strategic policy. As a matter of fact, it was this strategy of *Manifest Destiny* that became the pivoting axis of this entire world historical period.

The Historical Strategy of *Manifest Destiny*.

In brief, *Manifest Destiny* represents the westward development motion of Western Civilization following the model of republican sovereign nation-states in opposition to the eastern model of oligarchical imperial world domination. However, the American continental phase of that motion is sometimes wrongly associated with the "western cowboy" orientation of the criminal Andrew Jackson and his genocidal policy of ethnic cleansing against the Indians of the Cherokee Nation during the first half of the nineteenth century. This Jackson crime against humanity was an actual British imperial subversion of the *Manifest Destiny* strategy, whose name was made infamous under the false democratic flag of a British asset journalist, John L. O'Sullivan.

The original American phase of the *Manifest Destiny* strategy can be properly identified much earlier, when representatives of Cotton Mather and William Penn met to unite their forces in New York City, during the fall of 1689, to retaliate against the Count of Frontenac-led Indian massacres of several American colonial towns. This is where a decision was made by the Americans to defend their colonies by launching an invasion of Canada with an attack against Québec City in 1690. The defensive nature of William Penn's intention had already been shown through his peace treaty with the Shackamaxon Indians, according to which it was agreed that the Indians could sell-off their lands at a remarkably fair price. Penn considered that good business was better than conquest.

The irony, therefore, is that the claim to fame of the American leader of this Canadian expedition, William Phipps, does not come from Count of Frontenac's pompous reply to his call for surrender: "I will respond with the mouth of my cannons!" Phipps' real claim to fame was rather established by the fact that his presence before the ramparts of Québec City, in 1690, was coming from the American strategy of *Manifest Destiny*, which had been decided during the first Congress to ever unite the nine American colonies in 1689, and to finance their invasion independently of Great Britain. Let us look a little closer at the two sides of this ironic coin.

On the one hand, under the guise of a "religious war," against the Americans initiated by the French regime of Frontenac and his Venetian-deployed Jesuits in Canada, the British-Dutch effort of England's so-called "King William's War" (1689-1697), including his apparent sponsoring of the 1690 attack on Québec City, was also a Venetian deployment aimed at destroying the *Manifest Destiny* strategy of America, as well as destroying its corresponding Colbertian economic development orientation in Canada at that time. The two opposite oligarchies had the same objective: contain the American colonies on the Eastern shore of the Atlantic. Although this French and Indian War appeared to be only a side show of the larger theater of Venetian instigated "religious warfare," known as the "War of the Grand Alliance" (1688-1697), itself being fought in Europe at the same time against the *follie des grandeurs* of Louis XIV, the real objective of that Grande Alliance War against France was for the British to conquer the whole of America. Ironically, Phipps, a commoner who was the youngest of a Kennebeck family of 26 children, was not the best choice to carry out that imperial mission for the British-Dutch oligarchy.

On the other hand, the same William Phipps, who was to be appointed the first Royal Governor of Massachusetts, two years later (1692) by William III of Orange, actually represented the Massachusetts Bay Colony of the Puritans led by Increase and Cotton Mather, and was fighting against all forms of oligarchism, be they British, Dutch, or French. From the standpoint of the Americans, this was not a religious war. The Massachusetts Bay Colony had already built an anti-oligarchical sovereign self-governing colony of the people by and for the people on the East Coast of America. However, French-colonial Canada stood in the way of that purpose. As a matter of fact, during its entire history, at the exception of a very brief Colbertian moment of optimism, Canada has been the great exception to the hemispheric republican strategy of *Manifest Destiny.*

On the American side, the intention of fighting the French and Indian War (1689-1697) against Frontenac was aimed at consolidating the historical alliance of a Mather-Penn leadership among the nine American Colonies. At the New York Congress of 1689, some other crucial development occurred. Both Penn and the Mathers, in agreement with the General Court of the Puritan church, appointed John Wise as chaplain under the command of William Phipps. John Wise later wrote a very unique paper called *Vindication of the Government of New England Churches* (1717). The paper was obviously written in the spirit of Leibniz and explicitly in congruence with Plato's conception of the Democratic Republic of Athens. Though it was written for establishing the government of the Puritan Church of Massachusetts, John Wise's paper also represented the framework for a civil constitution of the New England colony. It can also be considered as the first blueprint for the American Constitution.

The purpose of the war against Canada was to break the barrier of the Appalachian Mountains against the French territorial claims over Western America. Following the first New England federation council of 1689, held in New York, the idea of Penn and of Mather was to develop the coal and iron mining industries including canal infrastructure capabilities for shipping American goods from within the continent throughout the world. This was exemplified by the Saugus Forges of Massachusetts, which represented the type of physical economic system that was then funded by the first public credit system known as "script," the paper-money forerunner to the Alexander Hamilton constitutional credit system. The same American credit system required for getting out of the current worldwide collapse of the financial system.

This original New England federation Congress of 1689 was in reality the very first United States Congress. Their intercolonial action led to the first intercolonial military deployment independently of Great Britain. So, from the standpoint of universal history, the break with the British oligarchical system seems to have started in that New York Congress. Up until that time, all nine of the American colonies were independent of one another, some even hostile to each other. Each had its own governing ways and its own problems to solve with respect to Britain. But, after that date, they all had a common goal: get rid of oligarchism and implement *Manifest Destiny*. This was the first historical opportunity they had to act together. They did, and the idea of a United States of America was born! As Graham Lowry showed in *How The Nation Was Won*, this decisive moment coincided with the successful ouster of the tyrannical king James II supported Andros regime (1688-89) in the New England colonies and the subsequent creation of an economically viable and independent New England movement seeking western expansion.

As a result of the first French and Indian War (1689-1697), all of New France extended through the entire eastern region of the Mississippi, preventing all of the American colonists from going west. The contested territory was located between the Great Lakes and the Gulf of Mexico and between the Appalachian Mountains and the Mississippi River. This Venetian-Jesuit-run French containment of the American colonies from Canada was the same strategy the British had later taken up for themselves. This diabolical and phony religious war originating from Canada had to be broken up.

Almost a century later, it was also the attempt to stop the Americans from going west and pursue their *Manifest Destiny* strategy that led the British to launch the *Seven Years War* (1756-1763) against France. This war also coincided in the United States with a second French and Indian War (1754-1760) against the Americans. In 1749, a group of Virginia businessmen had already secured claims of over 500,000 acres of land over the Appalachian Mountains into the Ohio River Valley, and were making plans to settle this region, and beyond, when the French blocked this new expansion effort. The building of forts and outposts by the French along the Ohio River was aimed at stopping this western American development. This is the time when the young George Washington was sent to build an American fortification in the same region, an action that the French used as a pretext to launch their second French and Indian War. Thus, the great leap across the Appalachians into the Ohio Valley had become the centerpiece of the economic self-development of the newly rising American nation-state Republic.

The American threat of expansion over the so-called 1763 Proclamation Line had been the explicit motive for the British to declare a second war against France. Again, this apparent larger European conflict

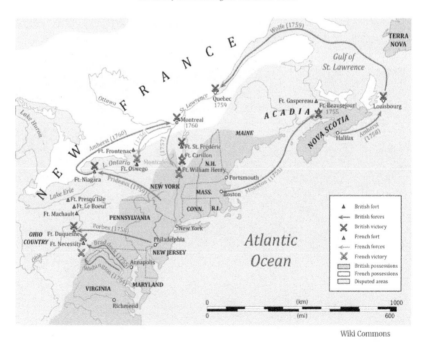

Wiki Commons

Top: North American territories prior to the British victory over France in 1763

Below: Key battles during the Seven Year's War

Wiki Commons

also had the same primary objective that William III of Orange had, and that was to conquer the whole of the American continent for the British East India Company. However, this time around, it was William Pitt and not William Phipps, who conquered Québec City, in 1759, and his intention was to have the British Hudson's Bay Company take over the French Ohio Valley before the American colonists did. The maritime power developed by Venice during the four British Dutch wars (1652-1684) had to be secured around the Anglo-Dutch faction later to be known as the British Venetian Party whose deadly threat was not located in Europe at all, but in America's *Manifest Destiny* development strategy.

The concept underlying Manifest Destiny can actually be traced back to 700 BC, before Solon of Athens, the Pythagoreans and the Platonic Academy, and how it was originally centered on the Greek efforts to save their civilization from the Eastern dominance of the Persian oligarchical model. Greek civilization was almost destroyed by the bestializing policy of oligarchism and its use of sophistry and evil priesthoods, such as the Persian Cult of Apollo at Delphi, during the Peloponnesian Wars. [1]

After the collapse of Athens, and the fall of the Roman Empire, *Manifest Destiny* was momentarily revived by the Ecumenical efforts of Charlemagne (800) in alliance with Haroun al Rashid's Islamic Renaissance and the collaboration of the Jewish Kingdom of Khazaria. Then, soon after the death of Charlemagne, the same type of Gnostic priesthood of Delphi was deployed by Venice in an attempt to destroy the Catholic Church through an ultramontane papacy run by the Jesuit, Benedictine, and Dominican orders. It was the Benedictine Hildebrand papacy (1073-1085), for example, which initiated the Crusades that nearly destroyed the whole of Western Civilization during three centuries by collapsing Europe into a dark age.

The *Manifest Destiny* strategy of Western Civilization was revived, again, when the great Cardinal Nicholas of Cusa centered his ecumenical efforts on uniting the Eastern Orthodox Church with the Roman Catholic Church in the West during the Council of Florence (1431-1445) and when he developed the principle of the *consent of the governed* as the basis for the sovereign nation-state in his *Concordancia Catholica*, which laid the basis for creating the first sovereign nation-state in France under Louis XI and in England under Henry VII. A few decades later, Cusa provided Christopher Columbus with the precious map coordinates of Toscanelli for seeking a Western territory that would protect itself against the oligarchy and the proverbial Eastern Persian Whore of Babylon.

Following in Cusa's footsteps, John Winthrop succeeded in solidly implanting a Puritan Republic in the Massachusetts Bay Company, the first self-governing popular Commonwealth in the world, led by Cotton Mather, who, with William Penn of Philadelphia created the first American Colonial Congress (1689), in order to decisively launch the American continental phase of *Manifest Destiny* against the Jesuit-Venetian control of Canada. According to American historian, Francis Parkman, the Jesuits were the leading proponents of the Venetian Ultramontane doctrine in America. As he put it, most aptly: *"The Jesuits, then as now, were the most forcible exponents of ultramontane principles. The church to rule the world; the Pope to rule the church; the Jesuits to rule the Pope: such was and is the simple program of the Order of Jesus, and to it they had held fast, except on a few rare occasions of misunderstanding with the Viceregent of Christ."*[2]

From the strategic standpoint of long waves of universal history, the colonial Congress of 1689 foreshadowed the War of Independence initiated against the British Intolerable Acts, including the Québec Act of 1774, which had been explicitly established against *Manifest Destiny*. This means that the William Phipps1690 invasion of Canada was the prelude to

Richard Montgomery's invasion of Montreal in 1775. Thus, 1689 reflected a critical *punctum saliens* in the American historical phase of the continued progress of *Manifest Destiny*; a progress that can be identified by about ten crucial markers since the birth of Western Civilization over 2,700 years ago:

700 BC: The Birth of Western Greek Civilization: Solon of Athens and Thales of Miletus;

350 BC: The Pythagorean and Platonic Academies;

0: The birth of Jesus of Nazareth and the origin of Christianity;

800: The Charlemagne ecumenical Jewish, Islamic, and Christian strategy and the Islamic Renaissance of Haroun al-Rashid;

1434: The Nicholas of Cusa Ecumenical Council of Florence;

1648: The Cardinal of Mazarin Peace of Westphalia;

1689: The first American Congress of Cotton Mather and William Penn in New York;

1776: The American Declaration of Independence followed by the Monroe Doctrine of John Quincy Adams;

1860: The successful Homestead Law and the US government funding of the transcontinental railroad by President Abraham Lincoln;

2007: The Franklin Delano Roosevelt legacy of the New Britton Woods and the Lyndon LaRouche Bering Strait Tunnel strategy linking the Americas with the Eurasian Land bridge.

2013-present: The renewal of the world land-bridge under the concept of the New Silk Road (Belt and Road Initiative) sparked by China which has created a new framework for development and cooperation alongside the BRICS, SCO and other Eurasian powers.

Thus, immediately after 1763, as cited by name in the Québec Act of 1774, it was the Merchant Adventurers at the Hudson Bay Company in Rupert Land who had consolidated themselves in order to prevent the

American strategy from going west, by taking full control of the territories east and west of the Mississippi. Thus, the western wing of the British East India Company had conquered three new territories, Canada, East and West

Top row (left to right): Solon, Plato, and Alexander the Great

Middle row (left to right): Charlemagne (by Durer), Nicholas of Cusa and Pierro Toscannell

Bottom row (left to right): Columbus, Cardinal Mazarin and John Winthrop

All images Wiki Commons

Florida, and the vast territories from the great Lakes to the Gulf of Mexico East of the Mississippi. This dangerous isolation of the American colonies became the *causus belli* that triggered the American Revolutionary War. The extension of the boundaries of Québec to the Ohio River by the Québec Act of 1774 was the worst of the series of intolerable Acts concocted by the British parliament against the Americans since 1763. The Québec Act was the proverbial drop that made the dam burst.

Clément Gosselin was made aware of a large part of this historical picture when he was recruited to the American cause in 1774. This was the general political context that surrounded his youth, in North America, and the strategy of Manifest Destiny was one of the primary motivations for him to recruit French-Canadians to the American war effort and to later propose to settle the Detroit area. Silas Deane and others had already made plans, as early as 1774, to have Americans secure the Detroit region. As reported by Henri Gosselin, a number of French-Canadian recruits had offered to become some of the first American settlers in the Detroit area, along the Huron River, and on the land that ran along the shores of Lake Erie. The purpose of that move was to explicitly counter the Québec Act of 1774.

Manifest Destiny vs. The British Québec Act of 1774

In the First Continental Congress of May 1774, it was Silas Deane who became the champion of the *Manifest Destiny* strategy. Nicknamed "Ticonderoga Deane" privately by his colleagues, Silas Deane was the Connecticut delegate who had most emphatically emphasized the necessity to relentlessly pursue the policy of *Manifest Destiny* by way of countering the Québec Act with an Invasion of Canada. On August 30, 1774, for instance, the Connecticut Courant (Hartford) reported, "*the Québec Act is the first in 200 years that establishes popery,*" and that by passing this intolerable Act, "*His Majesty has declared war on America.*" Shrewd as he was, after he had Ethan Allen and Benedict Arnold capture Fort Ticonderoga, Deane declared that it was done merely to prevent the British in Canada from accessing the ordinance of the fort and prevent them from making use of it against the Americans in case of a conflict.

The reason the Americans considered the Québec Act to be an act of war against America was because it excluded the right to self-government and gave Québec extended borders behind the Appalachians that went as far south and west as the Ohio and Mississippi rivers. It was, therefore, the continuation by the British oligarchy of the old French oligarchical policy.

In a letter to Samuel Adams, Deane warned against this Québec Act and its land grab and proposed a massive influx of new colonials in that region west of the Appalachians: "*This, or some such plan, will most effectually defeat the design of the Québec Bill, which if not broke thro' & defeated in some shape or other, will be the most fatally mischievous to the British Colonies of any Bill ever framed by the Ministry, or that may possibly ever enter into their Hearts To conceive of.*" In the same letter of November 13, 1774, Deane explained why the Québec Act represented such a grave danger for the strategy of *Manifest Destiny*:

"*The extending & fixing Settlements of Protestants Westward will not only bring about this wished-for event, but will be in future Days Our greatest Strength & Security. Another Tier as I may say of Colonies settled back of us will be, an inexhaustible resource to us, &c render Us humanely speaking invincible though the united Powers of the whole World should attack Us. Look at a Map, & see, the situation of the Countries between 40.° & 45.° through the Continent. This is the New England Inheritance, as fairly secured for them, by their Ancestors, as any one*

Acre they now possess, and once well settled with Our People, & their descendants, will give Law, not to North & South America alone, but to the World if they please.

"This will, & must be the most independent Country on the Globe, inland Seas or Lakes, and Rivers extending quite across the Continent in those parallels, and the Western extremity lands Us at the very Door, of the Treasures of the East, and The South. If the Contemplation of these future events gives Us pleasure every effort of Ours to ripen them if successful, in degree realizes them. This can hardly be called the pleasure of the imagination only, but rather the pleasure of anticipating great, & important realities, & such as are hastening on, & in the arrival of which, the happiness of Mankind is most deeply interested." [4]

It was because of that danger to their *Manifest Destiny* strategy that the signers of the Declaration of Independence denounced this Québec Act: "For abolishing the free System of English Laws in a neighbouring Province, establishing therein an Arbitrary government, and enlarging its Boundaries as to render it at once an example and fit instrument for introducing the same absolute rule into these Colonies."[5]

How the French-Canadians Lost Their Chance at Joining the American Revolution.

On October 26, 1774, the American Continental Congress sent an extraordinary letter *To the Inhabitants of Québec* . It was an invitation calling on them to join the American cause for independence.[6] The *Imprimerie de Fleury Mesplet* that Benjamin Franklin founded in Montreal, and which later became the printing house of the Montreal Gazette newspaper, published a few thousand copies of the invitation in 1774 by request of the Continental Congress of Philadelphia. This letter, translated into French, was turned into a pamphlet that became the primary organizing tool used by Clément Gosselin to recruit his Canadian associates to the Revolution. The Letter began as follows:

"*To the Inhabitants of the Province of Québec.*

"*Friends and fellow-subjects,*

"*We, the Delegates of the Colonies of New-Hampshire, Massachusetts-Bay, Rhode-Island and Providence Plantations, Connecticut, New-York, New-Jersey, Pennsylvania, the Counties of Newcastle Kent and Sussex on Delaware, Maryland, Virginia, North-Carolina and South-Carolina, deputed by the inhabitants of the said Colonies, to represent them in a General Congress at Philadelphia, in the province of Pennsylvania, to consult together concerning the best methods to obtain redress of our afflicting grievances, having accordingly assembled, and taken into our most serious consideration the state of public affairs on this continent, have thought proper to address your province, as a member therein deeply interested.*

"*When the fortune of war, after a gallant and glorious resistance, had incorporated you with the body of English subjects, we rejoiced in the truly valuable addition, both on our own and your account; expecting, as courage and generosity are naturally united, our brave enemies would become our hearty friends, and that the Divine Being would bless to you the dispensations of his over-ruling providence, by securing to you and your latest posterity the inestimable advantages of a free English constitution of government, which it is the privilege of all English subjects to enjoy.*

"*These hopes were confirmed by the King's proclamation, issued in the year 1763, plighting the public faith for your full enjoyment of those advantages.*

"Little did we imagine that any succeeding Ministers would so audaciously and cruelly abuse the royal authority, as to with-hold from you the fruition of the irrevocable rights, to which you were thus justly entitled.

"But since we have lived to see the unexpected time, when Ministers of this flagitious temper, have dared to violate the most sacred compacts and obligations, and as you, educated under another form of government, have artfully been kept from discovering the unspeakable worth of that form you are now undoubtedly entitled to, we esteem it our duty, for the weighty reasons herein after mentioned, to explain to you some of its most important branches.

"In every human society," says the celebrated Marquis Beccaria, "there is an effort, continually tending to confer on one part the height of power and happiness, and to reduce the other to the extreme of weakness and misery. The intent of good laws is to oppose this effort, and to diffuse their influence universally and equally."

"Rulers stimulated by this pernicious "effort," and subjects animated by the just "intent of opposing good laws against it," have occasioned that vast variety of events, that fill the histories of so many nations. All these histories demonstrate the truth of this simple position, that to live by the will of one man, or set of men, is the production of misery to all men.

"On the solid foundation of this principle, Englishmen reared up the fabrick of their constitution with such a strength, as for ages to defy time, tyranny, treachery, internal and foreign wars: And, as an illustrious author1 of your nation, hereafter mentioned, observes, −"They gave the people of their Colonies, the form of their own government, and this government carrying prosperity along with it, they have grown great nations in the forests they were sent to inhabit."[8]

"In this form, the first grand right, is that of the people having a share in their own government by their representatives chosen by themselves, and, in consequence, of being ruled by laws, which they themselves approve, not by edicts of men over whom they have no control. This is a bulwark surrounding and defending their property, which by their honest cares and labours they have acquired, so that no portions of it can legally be taken from them, but with their own full and free consent, when they in their judgment deem it just and necessary to give them for public service, and precisely direct the easiest, cheapest, and most equal methods, in which they shall be collected.

"The influence of this right extends still farther. If money is wanted by Rulers, who have in any manner oppressed the people, they may retain it, until their grievances are redressed; and thus peaceably procure relief, without trusting to despised petitions, or disturbing the public tranquility.

"The next great right is that of trial by jury. This provides, that neither life, liberty nor property, can be taken from the possessor, until twelve of his unexceptionable countrymen and peers of his vicinage, who from that neighborhood may reasonably be supposed to be acquainted with his character, and the characters of the witnesses, upon a fair trial, and full enquiry, face to face, in open Court, before as many of the people as chose to attend, shall pass their sentence upon oath against him; a sentence that cannot injure him, without injuring their own reputation, and probably their interest also; as the question may turn on points, that, in some degree, concern the general welfare; and if it does not, their verdict may form a precedent, that, on a similar trial of their own, may militate against themselves.

"Another right relates merely to the liberty of the person. If a subject is seized and imprisoned, though' by order of Government, he may, by virtue of this right, immediately obtain a writ, termed a Habeas Corpus, from a Judge, whose sworn duty it is to grant it, and thereupon procure any illegal restraint to be quickly enquired into and redressed.

"A fourth right, is that of holding lands by the tenure of easy rents, and not by rigorous and oppressive services, frequently forcing the possessors from their families and their business, to perform what ought to be done, in all well regulated states, by men hired for the purpose.

"The last right we shall mention, regards the freedom of the press. The importance of this consists, besides the advancement of truth, science, morality, and arts in general, in its diffusion of liberal sentiments on the administration of Government, its ready communication of thoughts between subjects, and its consequential promotion of union among them, whereby oppressive officers are shamed or intimidated, into more honorable and just modes of conducting affairs.

"These are the invaluable rights, that form a considerable part of our mild system of government; that, sending its equitable energy through all ranks and classes of men, defends the poor from the rich, the weak from the powerful, the industrious from the rapacious, the peaceable from the violent, the tenants from the lords, and all from their superiors.

"These are the rights, without which a people cannot be free and happy, and under the protecting and encouraging influence of which, these colonies have hitherto so amazingly flourished and increased. These are the rights, a profligate Ministry is now striving, by force of arms, to ravish from us, and which we are, with one mind, resolved never to resign but with our lives. [...]

"We do not ask you, by this address, to commence acts of hostility against the government of our common Sovereign. We only invite you to consult your own glory and welfare, and not to suffer yourselves to be inveigled or intimidated by infamous ministers so far as to become the instruments of their cruelty and despotism, but to unite with us in one social compact, formed on the generous principles of equal liberty and cemented by such an exchange of beneficial and endearing offices as to render it perpetual.

"In order to complete this highly desirable union, we submit it to your consideration whether it may not be expedient for you to meet together in your several towns and districts and elect Deputies, who afterwards meeting in a provincial Congress, may chose Delegates to represent your province in the continental Congress to be held at Philadelphia on the tenth day of May, 1775."[9]

One can only imagine that this briefing on inalienable rights and principles of the American System must have been at the center of every discussion and meeting that Captain Gosselin had in the process of organizing and recruiting his French-Canadian contacts to the war effort. This pamphlet was the most important organizing tool for developing young and alert Canadian minds just a year before the American War of Independence.

However, since by July 1775, the Continental Congress had gotten no response from Canadian political leaders to their invitation, and the Canadians had not sent a single delegate to the May 1775 convention in Philadelphia, the Continental Congress asked George Washington to make immediate preparations for launching an invasion of Canada with a simultaneous two-prong attack against the British occupation of both Montreal and Québec City. Clément Gosselin was ecstatic.

The idea of invading Canada had two subordinated objectives: **Plan A** was to defeat the British colonial army in Canada and make Canada the 14th colony of the United States. If this first objective were to fail, then **Plan B** was to prevent, by all means, the British located in Canada from invading the American colonies from the north. The choice of the month of September for the invasion was to facilitate the long march of the invading army through difficult terrain, and to delay any possible British reinforcement from England until after the winter months. The American troops had signed up for an expedition that was not to last more than four months in all, from September 1 to December 31, 1775.

Even though General Richard Montgomery succeeded in capturing Montreal by November of 1775, he had failed to capture the capital of Canada, Québec City, by the end of conscription of his troops. The invasion of Canada ended in a military defeat for the American troops, when Montgomery was killed in an almost suicidal assault against Québec City on the last day of the expedition, December 31, 1775, date at which the American forces were supposed to be back at Fort Ticonderoga.

The failure of this invasion reflected an important defeat for the Americans as well as for the population of Canada, which had been subjected to the scare tactics of British psychological warfare, and had been induced in rejecting the American call to freedom. Therefore, the Canadians missed the opportunity to participate in one of the greatest moments in human history, because they could not recognize the face of Providence when it came knocking at their door. Though the great majority of French-Canadians were favorable to the American Revolution, they missed their chance because they had not prepared themselves to fight for the establishment of self-government by and for themselves. Nor did they organize themselves to fight back against sophisticated British psychological warfare directed systematically against them.

The British oligarchy put up two major hurdles before the French-Canadians in order to prevent them from joining the Americans: one was political, the other religious. This Delphic operation was one of the sleaziest forms of religious interference into politics ever devised in history. As it were, this British ideological manipulation would have made the envy of the ancient Persian priesthood of the Oracle of Apollo at Delphi. The trick was to get the Canadians to buy their security at the cost of their liberty. How could this be done successfully since the great majority of the French-Canadians were known to be sympathetic to the Americans? The operation was concocted and very carefully crafted between the two top British intelligence operatives in Canada at that time: the Canadian Governor, Guy Carleton, and the Bishop of Québec City, Olivier Briand. The plan they concocted was a perfect fool's trap.

First, Carleton used the Québec Act to lure the French population into accepting the most generous offer that would guarantee them their

French-Canadian nationality, the official recognition of the Catholic religion (the Roman Catholic Church was already recognized in the Treaty of Paris of 1763), the right to their French language and customs, including the French system of the Civil Code, and the right for their Seigneurs (Lords) to levy taxes everywhere in the Seigneuries of Québec. How could the French-Canadians refuse such a gift all *wrapped up in fur*?

So, the Canadian leaders accepted this Québec Act, instead of the Invitation by the American Congress, knowing they were being given a poisoned gift in the form of sophistry, a real fallacy of composition, which they knew was a false security contract. Anybody with a little bit of brains knew this was a lie, and yet, they went along with it. They swallowed the whole thing, hook, line, and sinker because this was the easiest way to go along to get along. And, that is precisely the sort of security in which people will accept to live in the concentration camp of their own minds. Carleton thought: *"Who will dare complain after receiving everything they were asking for?"* The leadership of the population had agreed, consciously, to be fooled! The rest of the ignorant mass followed like the sheep of Panurge.

Even though the British were conscious that their psychological warfare gambit could succeed for the majority of the French population, they still required a guarantee to secure a consensus and to make a case against the recalcitrant few. This, for the British, became the decisive inflection point. Carleton was fearful that his coup might not succeed, if he were not supported in his maliciousness by bishop Briand; it would have been a total disaster So, he gambled everything on the weak flank of the French-Canadians, their religiousness! That is why the Bishop of Quebec provided Carleton with that ultimate guarantee. Briand used the one instrument that he could find to prevent the French-Canadians from joining the American Revolution:

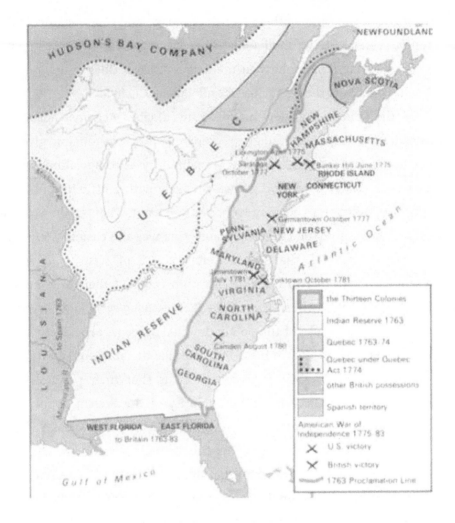

Entrapment of the American colonies by the extension
of Quebec under the Quebec Act of 1774. Note the 1763
Proclamation Line isolating the Americas.
Image from the Times Atlas of World History

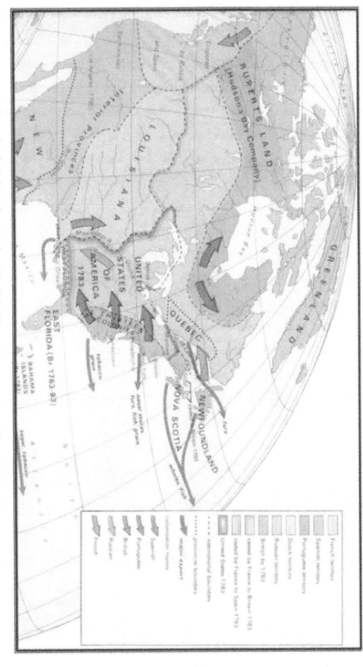

Map of Colonial North-America. The light blue section represents the French territories ceded to Britain and to Spain at the Treaty of Paris of 1763

EXCOMMUNICATION.

Therefore, in an open letter to all of the Churches of the diocese of Québec City, Briand warned that any supporter of the American Revolution would be excommunicated from the Catholic Church, would be denied the sacraments and the last rites, and would not be buried in sacred Church ground. That was a perfect Delphic trick, and it was used successfully to scare the great majority of the people.

Thus, British intelligence had devised a typical soft-cop-hard-cop scenario to capture the French population of Canada. This was a typical Mutt and Jeff police-state operation. Carleton was the soft cop and Briand was the hard cop. Carleton served the French with total security, with no need for self-government, and Briand served them with total insecurity, without exception. The choice for American supporters was either public humiliation or eternal damnation of their souls.

These were two fallacies of composition that Clément Gosselin had to fight against and defeat, if he wanted to win his own personal independence and recruit people to the revolution. This was the real price to pay for his political freedom. In order to better understand what was involved in Captain Gosselin's process of recruitment, let us go back, for a moment, to the time of the British conquest of 1759.

Gosselin Attacked by the British and the Church.

When the British came up the Saint Lawrence River with their fleet at the beginning of the Seven Years War, in 1759, they had planned to stop on the Isle of Orleans before proceeding to Québec City. In a sense, because they were living so close to Québec City, the Gosselin family had no choice but to be most directly involved in all such invasion events that were cast upon them from the proverbial outside world.

The Isle of Orleans, just 3 miles east of Québec City in the middle of the St. Lawrence, was itself indefensible, but was the best staging ground for preparing a siege of Québec City. The western part of the island was a perfect lookout point for identifying any military activity going on in the port and around the city's fortification. The Gosselin home was located on the eastern point of the island, itself an obvious choice for the British to take as their headquarters in this theater of operations before launching an attack on the city. So, regrettably, but inevitably, all of the inhabitants of the Isle of Orleans were always directly touched by such British invasions, and were forced to evacuate their island with each invasion.

Clément Gosselin's father, Gabriel Gosselin, one of the leading farmers on the Isle of Orleans, had been ordered by the Governor of Canada, the Marquis de Montcalm, to personally evacuate the island in expectation of the British fleet. Gabriel Gosselin was a Captain in the French militia and served as the military commander of the Island.

Although some people left courtesy messages in English, at the unlocked doors of their homes, welcoming the British to their food and shelters, in the hope that they would not destroy everything they had, in 1759, the British were quite barbaric and burnt down almost everything on the island. One of the few churches the British did not destroy completely was the Gosselin parish, Saint-Francois-de-Sales church, at the northeast point of the island.

This barbaric British behavior left an indelible mark on the 12-year-old Clément Gosselin. Clément and his family were very devoted Catholics. It was Gabriel Gosselin who had designed and built the Saint-Francois-de–Sales church that the British had partly destroyed. This is where Clément developed both his sense of spirituality and of carpentry. This is where he also discovered that one was not really separate from the other and that his love of God and his love of carpentry were made to develop together. Historian Henri Gosselin added the following important insight with respect to Clément's carpentry and his social compact with his Church.

"Such devotion on the part of the parishioners toward their churches and the religious authorities, at that time, was not unusual. The early habitants, in Québec lived in a simple fashion. For the most part, his house was devoid of decoration – both the interior and the exterior. His furniture was very plain. But his church was beautiful!

"Church after church was built on the Isle of Orleans, as well as along the entire north and south shores of the St. Lawrence River. Not only did these churches adorn the riverfront, but also parishes were established "en double rangée" (in double row). People took immense pride in their churches. They worked incessantly to build, maintain and repair those edifices, expending their money, which was scarce, and their goods and their labor.

"Their reward was having the opportunity to use the talents with which they had been endowed – and then having the satisfaction of seeing the fruit of their labor. Entering the church on Sunday morning and enjoying the art, which their own home lacked, they had a warm feeling of serving God, in whom their faith was so strong.

"To the French-Canadian, the parish was very important as a social unit. And, of course, the head of the parish and its chief animator was the pastor. The priest accepted the responsibility of mingling in both the spiritual and worldly affairs of his parishioners. Traditionally, he was the best-educated person in the parish – not only being the ultimate authority in theological matters, but also possessing a smattering of legal proficiency.

"The pastor has a capable dispenser of sound advice to families coping with a variety of problems. His opinion was sought by many of his parishioners before grave decisions were made. And in the confessional, he was the mediator between the sinner and his or her Maker – helping to restore the precious relationship that every parishioner craved with God." [10]

This is the way most of the generations of French-Canadians were brought up under the "discrete hand" of the parish priest, up until the so-called *quiet revolution* of the early 1960's, when the Canadian wing of the Congress for Cultural Freedom (CCF) broke up over 400 years of parish priest domination.

On December 8, 1775, Clément Gosselin was sitting and praying in the fourth pew of Sainte-Anne-de-la-Pocatiere church, when the parish priest, Father Pierre-Antoine Porlier, got up in the pulpit and pointed his finger angrily at him, declaring in an thunderous voice:

"Yes you, Clément Gosselin, will be excommunicated, from our holy Church. Msgr. Briand, our bishop, is warning you, and other rebels like you, that you must cease your seditious and mutinous behavior at once! Or else, suffer the consequences! If you join the American effort to try to expel our British conquerors from this land, do you know what will happen? It means that if you are mortally wounded in combat, you will be denied the last rites of the Church. No priest will hear your confession. And you will not be buried in sacred ground. Give that serious thought, Clément Gosselin! Your very soul is imperiled! And so are the souls of the innocent men of this village whom you are attempting to recruit." [11]

This did not come as a surprise. For almost a year, Clément had been recruiting friends and relatives to help the Americans. Everybody knew he was the top leader of the American cause in the Québec City region. However, the news of this public statement hit him on the head like a ton of bricks. He was not offended and he was not scared out of his wits, as Briand had hoped, but he was completely shocked and perplexed. He could not believe that his Bishop would go that far as to use religion for political ends. This was a most unbelievable and unprecedented religious intrusion into politics on the part of the top prelate of Canada. The moment of truth had come! Gosselin was being forced by his Bishop to choose between the unquestioned authority of his Church and his leadership role in the American Revolution, between the consensus of public opinion and the truth his own conscience. Gosselin made his choice!

Gosselin and the Creation of Two French-Canadian Congressional Army Regiments.

As in the case of all revolutionary change, only a handful of individuals are able to muster the courage to take the responsibility for what appears to be an impossible mission. Thus, only a small group of a few hundred French-Canadians joined the American Revolution. Most of them did not agree with the British oligarchical form of government and responded to the call of freedom and self-government. Some may have had more pragmatic reasons to join, but ultimately they saw in America the way to progress, the way to a better future for all.

It was after the American failure to take Québec City that Clément Gosselin's work began to be most important. He not only had the responsibility of assuring the safety of the remaining American troops traveling back during the winter months, but also of continuing his recruitment despite the failure of Plan A, to make Canada the 14th colony. His work was just beginning. From January 1776, the plan to prevent a British invasion from Canada, that is Plan B, had begun and the Americans were making their way back to Trois Rivieres, and from there to Montreal.

For Gosselin, plan B had become an additional part of his mission. The new recruits were no longer simply joining for a show of support, but to fight along side the Americans for the duration of the war. A new and more serious commitment to *Manifest Destiny* had to be taken for the rest of their lives. Those French-Canadian recruits had not merely become ideologically anti-British, but they had also become culturally American patriots.

At the same time, by 1776, British propaganda against Americans had taken a new twist and had escalated in Canada, when Carleton published a French translation of the *Letter to the British People* drafted by John Jay for the Continental Congress, in which the Catholic Church was strongly insulted and slandered. Some Canadians considered this to be double talk on the part of the Continental Congress. However, for Clément, this was understood as part of American psychological warfare to also wake up the British population.

Even though some of the new French-Canadian contacts and recruits were momentarily destabilized by the slanders and were offended by the attacks of the Continental Congress against the Catholic Church, Clément realized that in every war, both sides exaggerate their propaganda and lie to obtain the desired effect. He understood that what Carleton was doing was merely using the Congress *Letter to the British People* as counter-propaganda against the French population of Canada.

For the Americans, the plan A to make Canada the 14th colony had all of the appearance of having been abandoned and they had to secure their backs as they were marching south to Fort Ticonderoga, where the invasion had started seven months earlier. In March of 1776, the Canadian Militia in Trois Rivieres refused to march against the Americans, and by the time the Americans had reached Montreal, Clément had recruited several hundred new men. One of Montgomery's junior officers, Captain

Moses Hazen, proposed to the Commandant of the remaining American forces, Colonel Benedict Arnold, the creation of a new Canadian regiment.

By April of 1776, the American troops began to move south to Lake Champlain and, since the recruitment of French-Canadians was working so well, Benedict Arnold reportedly sent a request to the Continental Congress for raising two Canadian regiments of 1,000 men each, one of which would be led by Moses Hazen and the other by James Livingston. The Congress agreed.

Moses Hazen, a puritan from Massachusetts, was originally a junior officer in the British Army who had fought on the side of the British during the siege of Québec in 1759. After settling in Montreal as a Justice of the Peace, he began speculating to acquire properties in New Hampshire, Vermont, and along the Richelieu River at Fort St. John. It was Hazen who warned Carleton that Benedict Arnold had made a pre-invasion incursion at fort St. John with Nathan Allen, in May of 1775. Hazen was originally a British informant.

But then, during the summer of 1775, both the British and the Americans arrested Hazen for spying. Since his land was along the American invasion route, he was undecided as to which side would be more profitable for him. According to Henri Gosselin, *"He was sent an authorization by Governor Carleton (who considered Hazen a brave and experienced soldier) to raise troops and to join in defending Fort St. John against Montgomery's invading army."* It is not known if Hazen raised troops for the British at that time, but Montgomery did not live to tell the story as to why he was delayed for so long at Fort St. John before taking Montreal.

Hazen had also contacted General Schuyler, the American commander in charge of the invasion of Canada, and had warned him that such an invasion would be counter-productive and, therefore, attempted to stop the invasion of Montreal. Schuyler agreed with him at first, until

James Livingston, an American living in Chambly Québec, gave the general a more optimistic report, and convinced him of a possible successful invasion. As a result, Schuyler decided to go ahead with the invasion plan led by General Montgomery and gave Livingston the command of the First Canadian Regiment.

In 1775, Hazen was arrested by the Americans as a British spy, but only to be released again and arrested one more time by the British who, this time, brought him to Governor Carleton in Montreal, just before Montgomery took the city. Historian, Henri Gosselin, reported that Hazen had also been found on the same ship that carried Carleton to a successful escape from Montgomery's grip in Montreal. It is not known as to when and where Hazen made his Damascus conversion, but he did, and he ended up joining the Americans for good in the spring of 1776.

In March of 1776, the Continental Congress promoted Hazen Colonel and gave him the command of the Second Canadian Regiment in George Washington's Colonial Army. All of the recruits of Clément Gosselin now had an official accepted place and mission in the American Revolution, but the British confiscated all of Hazen's lands and properties in Iberville Québec as well in St. John on the Richelieu. The quota for the two regiments was high, that is, 2,000 French-Canadians, and Clément was not sure he was going to achieve that goal. He did not. According to Henri Gosselin:

"By the end of February (1776), 150 French-Canadians had enlisted in Hazen's regiment. And by the end of March, the number had grown to 250 recruits. Many were French soldiers who had remained in Canada following the conquest in 1759. However, the regiment was plagued by desertions – recruits who left shortly after collecting their enlistment bonuses.

"Edward Anctill concentrated on the Québec region – yet he barely managed to recruit five French-Canadians by mid-February. Clément Gosselin and Germain Dionne angered their pastor, Father Porlier, by enlisting several men in the La Pocatiere region. In Kamouraska, Pierre Ayotte succeeded in signing up a number of volunteers for Hazen's regiment.

"By April (1776), Livingston's first Regiment totaled 200 Canadian volunteers recruited from Trois-Rivieres to Kamouraska. However, they were well short of their projected 1,000 volunteers per regiment." [12]

Moreover, the Dictionary of Canadian Biographies further confirmed Gosselin's recruitment drive as follows:

"From January to May 1776 he (Clément Gosselin) traveled throughout the various parishes on the south shore of the St Lawrence from Pointe-Lévy (Lauzon and Lévis) to Sainte-Anne-de-la-Pocatière, recruiting volunteers for the Congressional troops. In this task he was aided by his father-in-law, Germain Dionne, who furnished clothing and supplies to the new recruits. Gosselin also called and presided over parish meetings for the election of militia officers, to whom he delivered Congressional commissions. Moreover, from the steps of the churches he read the orders and proclamations issued by the Americans, and he sometimes even forced the king's officers themselves to read them. Together with Pierre Ayotte, a habitant from Kamouraska who was equally devoted to the revolutionary cause, Gosselin organized a system of bonfires, under close guard, to warn the Americans of any approaching British ships." (Pierre Dufour and Gerard Goyer. [13]

A year later, in 1777, Captain Gosselin went back to La Pocatiere to sell his properties and was arrested and imprisoned in Québec City with his brother Louis and his father-in-law Germain Dionne. In the spring of 1778, all three were released and both Louis and Clément rejoined the Second Canadian Regiment in White Plains New York. Their regiment had been dubbed the *Congress' Own Regiment* (COR).

Just before France had joined the war, in 1778, the two Canadian regiments included a total of 450 French-Canadians. The Second Canadian

Regiment, to which Clément and Louis Gosselin belonged, was later deployed in the famous battles of Brandywine, Germantown, and Yorktown.

The regiment had also constructed a military road from Newbury Vermont to Hazen's Notch in northern Vermont in preparation for a second invasion of Canada to be led by General Lafayette into the Richelieu River Valley. This noisy affair in the underbelly of Québec had the British totally scared and convinced that the Americans were preparing a second invasion. In no time at all, Captain Gosselin had circulated the news of the French taking back Canada with the Americans all over Montreal, Trois-Rivieres, and Québec City. However this second invasion was not to materialize.

Nonetheless, Gosselin kept that threat of invasion very much alive and his counter-intelligence signals to the British were very effective in keeping the Canadian British forces on their toes in the Montreal, Trois-Rivieres, and Québec City garrisons during the entirety of the war. Gosselin had made Plan B for the invasion of Canada a complete success. One look at the 6 year deployments of the COR regiment in the northeastern part of the American colonies, from Québec City 1775 to Yorktown 1781, clearly shows why the British stayed put in Canada. This activity was also recorded in a letter from Captain Gosselin to the Continental Congress revealing that George Washington's French-Canadian had been responsible *"for the gathering of intelligence in Canada on three different occasions between 1778 and 1780, at the request of his Excellency (George Washington), the Count d'Estaing, and the Marquis de Lafayette."* [14]

On June 29, 1781, General George Washington promoted Colonel Hazen to Brigadier General. On October 4, General Hazen was ordered by Washington to bring his regiment for siege duty at Yorktown and serve as Brigade Commander under Lafayette during the Battle of Yorktown. On October 13, Captain Gosselin, was severely wounded in the leg by a piece of wood flying from a cannon ball explosion, while building a protective rampart on the Yorktown battlefield. So, it was from a stretcher that Captain Gosselin watched proudly the defeated British army march out of their Yorktown fortifications, on October 19, 1781. The Second Canadian Regiment was among the mile long lines of American and French troops facing each other while the defeated British troops of General Cornwallis marched silently between them. Cornwallis, as a typical superior British officer, was so humiliated that he refused to march out with his men.

When the two Canadian Regiments were discharged after the war, the Gosselin brothers, Hazen, and the other French-Canadians all received the gift of lands in Northern New York State. Most of them remained in America and became American citizens. After the Second Treaty of Paris of 1783, Clément Gosselin was promoted Major and received 1,000 acres of land for his services, which he sold soon after. Like Cincinatus, Gosselin returned to his carpenter's trade and lived in Saint Luc until 1815. Then, he sold his property for the last time and moved with his whole family to the Lake Champlain valley, where he had been given a land grant. He died in Beekmantown, New York, on March 9, 1816.

Conclusion: The Nominalist Crime of Pragmatism.

The fallacy of excommunication by Bishop Briand worked exactly like the fallacy of the Québec Act by Governor Carleton. Both actions were insidious means of luring the French-Canadian into a secured paddock and to have them put on, willingly, their own mental shackles. They were the wrong means to get to an apparently acceptable and practical end. They were both pragmatic ways to get people to *go along to get along.* That was precisely the pragmatism that Benjamin Franklin had attacked when he said: *"those who would sacrifice liberty for security deserve neither."* This is the proof that the British policy of pragmatism is for animals and is never fit for human consumption.

So, in a nutshell, Clément Gosselin and his friends had to fight, during the entirety of the American War of Independence, against two pragmatic fallacies of composition, one was the real "false" excommunication, and the other was the real "false" Québec Act. I say "false" because both of these were, in reality, fallacious instruments of coercion, that is, lies. Simply look at how the fallacy worked with Carleton:

Carleton said to the British Parliament: *"The success of my Québec Act policy depends on cheating the French-Canadians of their freedom."*

Is he telling the truth? Yes and No!

Yes, he is sincere in saying that the French-Canadians will join the Americans if he does not give them a semblance of freedom. No, he is lying because he has no moral right to do something wrong for what he thinks will yield him a good practical result.

As for Briand, he was also an untruthful sophist because he used the instrument of excommunication in a case where excommunication did not apply. No one had committed heresy. So, both Carleton and Briand acted out of malice, because both of them had no right to speak in flagrant disregard to the truth. As a result of such a nominalist crime of pragmatism, the Canadian people were never liberated nor acquired sovereignty.

However, in this same passionate spirit as Benjamin Franklin's, Father Laurent Gosselin, MSC, a Catholic missionary of the Sacred Heart, to whom Henry Gosselin dedicated his book, summarized the case of Clément Gosselin succinctly and quite aptly when he wrote:

"There was in Clément and Louis Gosselin, I think, an innate sense of justice which may not have made them popular with their superiors – religious or other – unless these shared the same passion for justice and fairness towards all. This attribute has driven many – like Major Clément and the French-Canadians he recruited – to give their all for the promotion and defense of the noblest causes. By their action, they greatly contributed to the success of the American Revolution. We have every right to be proud of the contribution that Clément and Louis and the French-Canadians made in assisting the Americans gain their freedom and independence." [15]

Here, Father Gosselin had a very true and profound insight into the soul and mind of Clément Gosselin, in the simultaneity of his temporal eternity with him, because he was able to transcend centuries to rediscover and relive, himself, the universal physical principle of love of mankind, *agape*, that provided the flame for Clément's revolutionary passion. This flame is still alive deep in the souls of all Canadians today, but, the true question of independence is: how many of them are willing, like Clément Gosselin, to break with the consensus of popular opinion and carry the newly rekindled beacon of hope that Lyndon LaRouche has provided for them as the next step to be taken in the historical course of *Manifest Destiny*? How many Canadians can we recruit for the purpose of carrying this shining beacon westward, through the dark but liberating pathway of the Bering Strait Tunnel, in order to guarantee a better future for all of mankind?

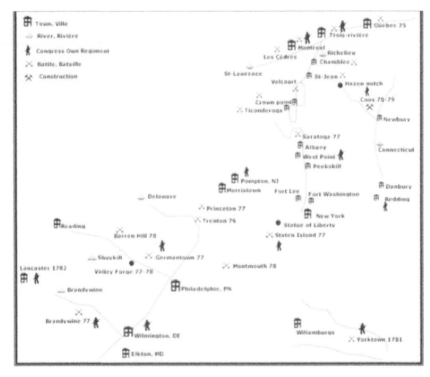

Above: Deployments of the Congress Own Regiment (COR) led by Colonel Moses Hazen and his French-Canadian troops during the war of Independance

Below: John Trumbel's rendition of the surrender of General Cornwallis' troops on October 19, 1781. American, French and Canadian trops look on.

CHAPTER IV - THE GOSSELIN 1778 LETTER TO GEORGE WASHINGTON

During the course of 1777, one year after the beginning of the American Revolutionary War, British General John Burgoyne, head of the British United Imperial Loyalists located in Canada, designed an ill-fated scheme to invade the American colonies from Quebec by moving south via Lake Champlain, capturing Ticonderoga, and attempting to isolate New England from the southern colonies by joining forces with another British army under General William Howe, Commander in chief of the British expeditionary forces in the American colonies, whom he expected to join coming from New York. His lack of understanding strategy, and his overconfident belief that he could win this war with superior forces, led him to be trapped, in fact, by superior American strategy.

Burgoyne, who was given a large army from England, committed what may have been the biggest blunder of the American Revolutionary War. He was led to believe that he would get the support of American Indians and of American Loyalists, but failed to realize that after a few nominal victories at Fort Ticonderoga, he was to be hemmed in by the superior strategy of American Major General Horatio Gates and General George Washington. After several attempts to break through the American lines at Saratoga, on October 17, 1777, Burgoyne was forced to surrender his whole army of 6, 200 British troops. That American victory proved to be a crucial turning point in the Revolutionary War. Four months later, France recognized the just cause of the American colonies and entered the war against the British on February 6, 1778.

Clément Gosselin was the principal French-Canadian leader who joined the American Revolution in order to upset the British war plans and tilt the balance in favor of George Washington.

A Sketch of Clément Gosselin

Clément Gosselin joined the American Revolution in Quebec City after the Second Continental Congress had issued a letter inviting Canadians to join the American Revolution. Gosselin was recruited when the Continental Army invaded Quebec on December 31, 1775.

From the beginning of January 1777, Gosselin organized and recruited Canadians to join the Americans. On the south shore of the Saint Lawrence River, from Lauzon and Levis to Saint-Anne-de-la- Pocatière, Gosselin recruited about 150 volunteers to join the Congressional troops. According to a Canadian biography of Gosselin online; "Gosselin also called and presided over parish meetings for the election of militia officers, to whom he delivered Congressional commissions. Moreover, from the steps of the churches he read the orders and proclamations issued by the Americans, and he sometimes even forced the king's officers themselves to read them. Together with Pierre Ayotte, a habitant from Kamouraska who was equally devoted to the revolutionary cause, Gosselin organized a system of bonfires, under close guard, to warn the Americans of any approaching British ships." [Our Most Popular Biographies]

In March of 1776, Gosselin became a captain in the Moses Hazen 2nd Canadian Regiment after he had recruited a group of about 150 pro-American Canadians who joined the Americans and defeated the pro-British Canadians at the Battle of Saint-Pierre, south of Quebec City. After the Congressional troops lifted the siege of Quebec and retreated south to New England, Gosselin did not follow his regiment, and instead, went underground for a period of fifteen months in order to recruit silently for the American effort.

In August of 1777, Gosselin sold his land, but was shortly later arrested and imprisoned in Quebec City. In the spring of 1778, Gosselin was liberated and rejoined his regiment at White Plains, New York, accompanied by his brother Louis and his father-in-law, Germain Dionne.

In 1778, the Hazen COR was given the task of opening a road for the purpose of invading Canada from Newbury VT., to the border of Quebec. This was part of Gosselin's spying mission whose purpose was to spread the rumor of an imminent American invasion accompanied with French troops commanded by General Lafayette. This invasion never took place and, therefore, the strategy completely succeeded in confusing the newly appointed British Governor of Canada, Frederick Haldiman, who was afraid to see a majority of the French Canadians rally to the French troops in America.

That fear was based on George Washington's recruiting Captain Clément Gosselin to be his primary spy whose role was to both evaluate the strength of the British forces north of the border, and disseminate in Canada the propaganda that the Americans were preparing an invasion via the same route that had proven fatal to Burgoyne. The road building from

Vermont to Quebec was meant as a diversion to keep the British guessing. The Washington strategy was the same as the LaRouche strategy, today: the aim is recruiting Canadians to fight for their freedom alongside the Americans. The letter that Captain Gosselin wrote to General Washington to inform him of the Canadian situation is a true testimony to the superior strategy of George Washington and of the American System over the British Imperial System.

The original French letter of the Gosselin brothers to George Washington can be found at the National Archives of the Rotunda University of Virginia Press: http://founders.archives.gov/. The original document is here transcribed under the title TO GEORGE WASHINTGTON FROM BRIGADIER GENERAL JACOB BAYLEY, 23 NOVEMBER 1778, and is followed with two intelligence reports in French which I have also translated below. Gosselin was in Newbury Vermont, when he wrote this letter to General Washington and was probably included in the diplomatic pouch of Jacob Bayley.

[For the sake of the modern reader, 18th century spellings have been updated and name corrections have been made where they were mis-spelled in 1778 original. In the letters written in French, no such corrections have been made —ed]

TO GENERAL GEORGE WASHINGTON FROM BRIGADIER GENERAL JACOB BAYLEY

Newbury, Vermont, November 23rd, 1778

Two Day Since Capt. Gosselin, Lt. Gosselin, Capt. Travisie and Enoch Hall arrived here from Canada which Place they left the 4th Instant, Capt. and Lt. Gosselin from Laubener Eighteen Leagues from Quebec, Capt. Travisie and Enoch Hall from St Francois, their accounts of the Situation of affairs In Canada I enclose wrote by Capt. Gosselin In French as I Apprehend the Truth would appear by their Verbal and written account(1) – they all agree that the Numbers in Canada of British force of all Sorts dos not amount to more than 3700 men that not more than 700 had arrived in Canada the last Season nor Could any arrive after they left that Country as it froze Hard at that time, that the Canadians were generally In favour of our Cause that the Priests were Silent, one assisted them much, Chief of the Force in Canada is in the District of Montreal, and were fortifying at Sorel where Head Quarters were and many Barracks, that the Canadians are not Disarmed In general but are not allowed to purchase any ammunition nor keep any without Special license, they are Impatiently waiting for our Coming, they Say that four Hundred men will Cut of the Communication between Quebece and Sorel if they fall in at St Nicolas(2) which is Eighteen miles below St Francois where the Communication is open from this Place, wheat Plenty at 5/pr bushel, pork & beef not So plenty but, they think Enough may be had for the army Mr. Hall Is one of our Inhabitants and Gives the Same accounts as the French, assures me that the French are very friendly that he was in Company with French officers that was in the works at Sorel they tell him their is but twenty Cannon a Small Fort and are making an Entrenchment from Sorel to the River St Laurence but no fortification on the two Sides next the River's.

The Indians begin to Come, in and mean never to go to Canada until the British are drove out, Capt. Travisie has been of great Servise to us this is the fourth time he has been in Canada Since he was drove out of that Country by the British, also Joseph Lewes has assisted us very much I wish they might be Recommended to the Commander of the Expedition, I am with the Greatest Regard your Excellency's most obedient Humble Servant

Jacob Bayley

The enclosed letter from Capt. Clément and Lt. Louis Gosselin to "Son Excéllence L'honorable Géorge Washington Général en chef Detoutte L'amerique &&&," dated "a Quas Ce 23 octobre 1778"

"Comme ayant été deputé pour aller en Canada pour donner L'intelligence au Canadiens des nouvelles Certainnes de l'ameriques, et examiner ensuitte ce quil Sy passoit, nous avons prie La Liberté de vous Les exposé, avec verité Sans aucun deguisement ny exagération.

"Le Contenu est, et de la façon que nous avont agit pour Les Savoir qu'etant arivé Le vinthuit d'octobre a l'abée St antoinne, nous nous Sommes informé ou étoit Les gardes afin de pouvoir agir a la cause pour laquel nous y'étions, Comme personnes ne vouloit dans aucune façons nous parler de Crainte des torés ni mesme nous donner aucune provision aussi par Crainte destre vue et découvert, mais les nouvelles que nous leurs avons anoncé de la Réunion de la france avec lamerique leurs a donné de la hardiesse pour nous donner des provissions, Cela étoit avec grand besoin car alors il y avoit trois jour que nous n'avions pas mengé.

"Quant il a été question de trouver des personnes pour decouvrir dévant nous ce Quil Se passoit afin de n'estre point surpris par les gardes pour aller jusqua l'aubinier a dishuit lieu de Québec, nous avons été dans l'obbligation de donner une Comission de Capt. a un nomé boiverd pour l'encouragér le Conoissant pour un homme de probité quil La accepté Comme venant de vostre Respectable part, Cette homme aussitot Remplie de Courage se voyant ainsi Revetue dès ordres de l'honorable Congréss nous a fourni les moyens pour avoir un découvreur pour marcher devant nous, Comme le jeune homme qui étoit pour faire Cette marche Cragnoit d'estre aresté nous Luy avont fait une passe du Général de la province par La quel il luy étoit permis d'aller oubon luy sembleroit, par Ce moyen nous Sommes parvenus de nous Rendres jusque chez Monsieur gaciens Curé de l'aubinier, la étant, je luy ai demandé les nouvelles quil pouvoit y avoir Savoir le nombres des troupes le nom des Generaux et de la justice ainsi que du Reste, par le quel je l'ai prié de me donner le total de mes demande par Écrit mais quil ne les signeroit pas, de crainte que Nous ne fussions prit il m'en a donné un en Ces termes pour que je ne fusse point inquietté, ny luy nonplus Si aucas jusse été pris.

"Le voicis il ne me reste plus que trois milles livres, et Sept Cent que je pourai trouver de nouvéau, Quand aureste, il ne m'est pas possible, D'en faire Davantage je n'ai que quatre ou Cinq amis qui ne sont pas fort puissant et ne me peuvent, estre plus utils, que je ne Leurs puis estres, Messieurs Maban, donne [Dunn], et panet, sont dans le Cas dans faire, mais ces pour eux et non pour moy.

"En voicis l'explication

"Les trois milles livres dont il parle, Ce sont trois mille hommes, pour les armes, et Les autres Sept cens livres, est le Renfort qui est venu Cette anné en Canada, donc il ne Luy est pas possible d'enfaire d'avantage. Cest adire que tant que toré Royaliste et troupes quil ne sont que trois milles sept cens homes, les quatres ou Cinq amis quil a Ce sont de messieurs de la Robe qui tienne pour les ameriquains, et donc tous le clergée est a L'encontre, Monsieur Mabon &c. sont les noms des juges de Quebec, la ou il dit quil sont dans le Cas d'en faire, mais pour eux et non pour luy, Cest adire quil font Ce Quil peuvent pour gagner Les Canadiens, mais Quils ne le peuvent pas, par ce quils sont Dans une tres Bonne disposition pour joindre avec L'amerique, quoy quils se plaignent quil sont embandoné a la fureur de tous leurs ennemis, et Quils souffres les peinnes les plus Languissantes en esperant leurs delivrance, ne desirent Que l'arivée des ameriquains, afin de pouvoir estre armée Pour donner assistance, a leurs Libérateurs, Car ils ne leurs est pas permis d'avoir ny poudre ni bal Sous peinne de punitions Corporels, Ces Ce quils espêre avec L'armée quil doit y penetrer, quils leurs porteront toutte Les munitions necessaire pour Combatre, Ceux qui les font souffrir avec tant de rigeur, les meaux les plus facheux, la joie quils auroit alors, Leurs feroit oublier toutte Les peinnes quils ont enduré, sous la tirannie de l'anglois. il est Certain q'au quatre de novembre que nous avons partie de Canada quil ny avoit que le nombres des trouppes Cidessus mentioné, l'on tien Cela pour Certain parceque attendu que C'est sortie de la propre bouche des juges de Quebec, nous pouvont assurer avec Certitudde, quil n'est point arivé d'autre Renfort en Canada depuis nostre départ, Car yl y avoit Dejas des glaces quant nous en sommes partie, a moins que ce ne fut quelque extraordinairre, ce seroit alors Ce que l'on auroit jamais vue sils enfusent venu apres nostre depart, par Ce quil n'attendoit aucun securs Cette autonne de plus il est partie de Québec trentre Cinq navir qui sont chergé ditons du milleur bagage du pays, et quil s'envont a londres.

"vostre Exelence aura syl vous plais la bonté d'accepter nostres humbles Respest en vous supliant tres humblement d'avoir pitié deux et d'avoir la bonte de Nous accorder vostre protections Car nous avons appris en Canada que tous nos biens étoit saisie et que nos familles étoit à lamandicite et a la mercie dumonde Nous ne Cesseront de prier dieu pour vostre Concervations afin quil benisse Les armes de L'ameriques et tous les Généraux qui les Gouverne Les plus soumis De vos serviteurs".

Appended to the Gosselins' letter is a "*Rèponse des Observations que nous devions faires en Canada,*" signed by them and reading:

"A savoir ils Sont au nombres de trois milles Sept Cents hommes tant que trouppes Reglée toré et Royalistes, cela est Sortie, de La bouche des juges qui en Conversant avec monsieur gacien, Luy ont assurè Ce Cis pour Certain, et veritable.

"ils Sont venus Cette anné au nombres de Sept Cens, qui est le surplus des trois milles Sans en attendre d'autres Cette anné.

"les trouppes en canada Sont dans un tres movais état, surtout ceus qui Sont a St françois a l'abée St antoine et a nicollet, qui est le Regiment du Colonel Bernard, ils Sont presque nue, et Sans couverte ils Sont chez les habitans depuis St françois jusqua nicollette tant au Sud q'au nort au nombres de cinq Cent, et dans la ville de quebec l'on fait nombre de Soixante a quatrevint hommes de trouppes.

"Les Canadiens qui Sont Sous les armes n'ont point été forcé ils y Sont de bonne volontée a la Reserve de ceus qui y Sont pour les Corvèe.

"Ses toré Canadiens Sont dans la Croyance que les ameriquains n'entrerons jamais en Canada ou que S'yl parvienne a y entrer, quil Seront encore des mieux venu disant quil deffende leur bien et quil Soutienne les intérest d'une Couronne Sans vouloir Croire que la france porte Secour a lamerique, a cette effest, ils s'efforce a faire de leurs pis, et a s'enrichir au dépend de Ceus qui favorise le partie de la liberté et les font souffrir les indignitée les plus grandes et les charges de traveaux pour le Servise duroy afin de les faire périr, le clergé de Son Coté qui est apuyé par les puissances Britaniques Se font une gloire de tiraniser avec toutte la Rigeur dont ils sont Capable ceus quil traitte de rebels, et d'indigne destre a la Compagnie d'aucune honeste gens, a la Reserve de trois pere jesuistes, et de deux prestres, qui Sont, lepere la Brosse, le pere floquette, le perre germain, Monsieur trutau Curé de la paroisse de Kamouraska, e monsieur gacien Curè de la paroise de l'aubinier tous messieurs qui Se Sont Comporté avec des Sentiments due a leurs etat.

"Les Sauvages du Canada Sont dans une tres bonne dispositions pour les ameriquains, L'on ne fait nombres que de cinq du village St françois quil Sont torè, encore ne le Seroit yl pas, S'il n'etoit soulvé par les Canadiens torè qui les font peur ainsidire marcher Comme malgré eus et Comme par force.

"Le Général est monsieur harguiman, Son aide de Camp, C'est monsieur de lanoyer, le gouverneur est Monsieur tramahé [Cramahé], monsieur <can>ot est celuy qui donné l'indice de faire les ordres et pour les faire éxécuter avec toutte les cruautées imaginables, les nom des juges Sont Messieurs donne [Dunn], maban, Wlliam, panêt, et Monsieur boissèau greffiè.

"Les Blaid Sont a trois chelin édemis et quatres chelin.

"il y a des paroise qui ont été désarmé et d'autres qui ne l'ont point été les on disent quils avoit des ordres les autres disent le Contraire mais yl est bien Certain que les paroises audebas de Québec ont été désarmé entierement, mais C'etoit les Capitainnes qui le fesoit de leurs chef Sans ordre.

"les Canadiens, Ceus qui Soutienne pour l'amerique, qui est la plus forte partie, Sont dans une grande inquiétude, il Seroit bien tous charmé de joindre avec l'amerique, mais la crainte quils ont que les ameriquains ne puisse pas parvenir de les Soulager les empêchent d'eclatter, il murmure beaucoup que les nouvelles que l'on leur porte que Ce Sont des fauseté et disent que depuis le tempt que lon les f<ait> esperer Leur délivrance quil

Croyent que Cest pour semoquer d'eus, et que les ameriquains ne Sont pas Si Soutenu quil Le disent, mais cependant la joie quils ont de Savoir que la françe est Reunie avec l'amerique leurs donne une bonne idée de La Réusitte des ameriquains".

Also appended are the following observations by Capt. Joseph Traversie:

"Le Capt traversi apres avoir été arivé en canada a éxaminé jusqua sorel Ce qui Sy passoit yl Raporte que les anglois ont bâtit Soixante et dis maisons pour loger les troupes, et deus hongar de Cens pié chaque pour y mettre Des provisions en outre quils ont fait un Retranchement d'une Riviere a l'autre avec des forteresse.

"un nomé dépin luy a dit quil avoit été comendé dans cent Cinquante voitures avec Cinquante bateau pour aller a St jean, chacun murmure que Ces pour en decendre les munitions.

"il est partie aussi de laurel en deus brigade Six cens hommes pour aller du coté de St jean mais L'on ne sai pas pour quoy Cependant, on luy a assurè quil étoit arivé a montréal Cinquante blessé anglois dont on ne Sai pas d'ou il vienne, lon pense que ces deus brigade Sont en marche pour aller donner quelque Renfort.

"a St françois yl ny a que quarante hommes de trouppes Reglée pour y faire La garde tant a labée St antoine, a nicollette, a ma chiche a la pointe du lac et au trois Riviere, yl ne Sont Que cinq cent hommes qui est le Regiment du colonel Bernerd.

"De plus on luy a assuré qui Sont les voyageurs mesme qui ont été mener les Sauvages, que les anglois avait fait decendre de michel makina pour frapper Sur les ameriquains, mais quand yls ont été a montréal le gènèral harguiman n'a pas trouvé a propos de S'en Servir ils Luy on Rèpond que puis quil les avoit fait venir pour faire la guer quil vouloit la fairre que si ce n'etoit pas aus ameriquains que ce Seroit Sur eux ou quil leur donneroit cent piastres a chacun d'eus et quils étoit sept Cens homes quil faloit quil les fit Remener a leurs village, Messieurs les anglois on voulu faire les Resolu, mais les sauvages on comencé par en tuer trois ou quatres et il auroit Certainnement détruit tous le montréal Si pour les adoucir il ne euse pas chargé depresent, et tous ce quil demandoit afin de les apéser et pour S'endébarasser au plus vite, et les mesme voyageurs ont assurè, que les ilinois étoit prie et le detroit, et la barque qui voyage de michelmakina au dètroit Ces Ce quils ont assuré.

"Le pere germain qui est Curé a St françois luy a dit quil etoit Certain que les forteresse que les anglois fesoit a sorel, que C'etoit Simplement pour faire paroitre quil fesoit leurs possibles pour garder le canada, afin de fairre paroistre de tel depense au Roy, et que sitost quil voiroit paroistre les ameriquains quils ambandonneroit tous cela.

"En outre un nomé la grave marchand autrois Rivierre dit avoir vue embarquer dans les navirs tous les Canons qui venoit de St jean et quil Les envoyoit a Londres".

Clément Gosselin (1747–1816) and his brother Louis Gosselin (1744–1823), both of Quebec, were among the small number of Canadians who supported the American attack on that place in December 1775. During the first half of 1776, Clément served as a recruiter and propagandist for the revolutionary cause in Canada. In March 1776 he was appointed a captain in Col. Moses Hazen's 2d Canadian Regiment, but he spent much of the next eighteen months in hiding before being captured and imprisoned by the British in Quebec toward the end of 1777. Gosselin was released and rejoined his regiment at White Plains, N.Y., in the spring of 1778, and over the following two years he frequently snuck back into Canada to prepare the road for an American invasion that never came. He was wounded at the Battle of Yorktown in October 1781, and after leaving the army in June 1783 he settled for a time near Lake Champlain before returning to Canada in 1791, where he remained for the rest of his life. "Laubener" is Lotbinière, on the south bank of the St. Lawrence River about thirty-five miles southwest of Quebec. Enoch Hall (1736–1806) served during the war as lieutenant of a small party of rangers raised by Vermont for the defense of the frontier; in 1785 he became one of the pioneer settlers of Isle La Motte on Lake Champlain.

End of the Bayley report.

CAPTAIN CLEMENT GOSSELIN AND LIEUTENANT LOUIS GOSSELIN TO HIS EXCELLENCY, THE HONORABLE GEORGE WASHINGTON, COMMANDING OFFICER OF ALL OF AMERICA, November 23, 1778.

Sir,

Since we have been deputized by you to come to Canada and to give intelligence to the Canadians as to the latest news from America, and have been asked to report back to you on the situation in Canada, we have taken the liberty to expose to you the whole truth plainly and without any exaggeration.

When we arrived at Saint-Antoine-Abbé (on the Richelieu), on October 28, 1778, our purpose was to find out where the guards were located so that we could act in accordance with your plan . Even though no one wanted to speak to us in any way for fear of the Tories nor would give us provisions, also for fear of being observed and discovered; nevertheless, the news we gave them of the alliance that France was making with America finally gave them the courage to give us some provisions. This was much needed since we had had nothing to eat for three days.

When the time came for us to find people to tell us the situation that we faced so that we would not be recognized by the guards on our way to Lotbinière at eighteen leagues from Quebec City, we had to give a commission of Captain to a Mr. Boisvert in order to recruit him. We knew him to be a man of integrity, and he respectfully accepted the commission as if it came from you, and immediately, filled with courage as he considered that he had been vested with the powers of the honorable US Congress, he helped us to recruit a pathfinder to scout for us. But, because the young man who was to scout for us was afraid to be caught, we managed to get him a free pass from the Governor of the province which gave him the right to go anywhere he wished to go. Thus, we managed to arrive at Monsieur Gacien, the parish priest of Lotbinière.

Once there, I asked him what news he had about the number of troops, the names of the Generals, the head of the court system, and the rest of the information, which I asked him to give me in writing, but without his signature, in case we were to be caught. He agreed to write this report under these conditions so he would not have to worry if ever I got caught. Here it is:

"I only have three thousand pounds left and seven hundred more that I could find. As for the rest, it is not possible for me to do more, I only have four or five friends who are not very powerful and who are not more useful to me than I am for them. They are Mr. Maban, Mr. Dunn, and Mr. Panet, (qui sont dans le cas d'en faire), who are in a situation of hell, but for themselves and not for me."

Let me explain. The three thousand pounds refers to three thousand armed soldiers, and the other seven hundred pounds refer to the soldiers in reserve who came to Canada this year. It is not possible that there be a greater number than that. This means that the number of Tories or Royalists and their military force does not exceed three thousand seven hundred men. As for the four or five friends he has, they are judges and magistrates who are waiting for the Americans to come; and therefore, the whole clergy is against them. Mr. Mabon and the others are judges in Quebec City, where he said they are in a situation of hell, doing the best they can for themselves, but not for him. In other words, they are doing all they can to help the Canadians, but they are not successful, because they are getting ready to join the Americans.

Although they complain that they have been abandoned to the fury of their enemies and that they are suffering terrible pains while waiting to be rescued, they only desire to see the Americans arrive so that they can be given arms to support their liberators, because they have been forbidden to have any ammunition under pain of physical punishment.

What they hope is that the invading army will bring them all of the necessary ammunitions to fight those who are making them suffer the worst pains. The joy they will then be filled with will make them forget all of the sufferings they were made to endure under the tyranny of the English.

We are certain that when we left Canada on November 4th, there was no greater number of troops than we have mentioned above. We hold that to be certain because we got it directly from the mouth of the Quebec City judges. We can assure you, with certainty, that no other fresh supply of troops have entered Canada since our departure, because there was already ice on the rivers when we left. It would be an extraordinary occurrence if new troops were to have arrived after our departure, something never seen, because no new reinforcement was expected last fall, when thirty five ships were said to have left Quebec City harbor loaded with the best merchandise of the country in destination for London.

Please, your Excellency, accept our most humble respects in begging you to have pity on them and to give us your protection, because we have learned that all of our belongings had been seized in Canada and our families have been reduced to mendacity and are at the mercy of everyone. We will not cease to pray God to protect you and that he bless the arms of America and all of the generals that lead them. The most humble of your servants.

Signed: Captain Clément Gosselin and Lieutenant Louis Gosselin.

*Appended to the Gosselin brothers' letter is a **"RESUME OF OBSERVATIONS BROUGHT BACK FROM CANADA"**, and signed by them. It reads as follows:*

From a conversation that Mr. Gacien had with the judges of Quebec City, we have been given the total assurance that there are three thousand seven hundred regular Tory and Royalist troops in Canada. Aside from the seven hundred troops who came this year to be added to the three thousands already on duty, there is not expectation of any new ones this year.

The Canadian troops are in bad shape, especially those located at Saint-François, at Saint-Antoine-Abbé, and at Nicollet. They are the Regiment of Colonel Bernard, almost naked and without shelter. There are about five hundred lodged at farmers' homes from Saint-François all the way to Nicolet, on the South as well as on the North side. In Quebec City, there are another sixty to eighty troops.

The Canadians who are in arms have not been forced to take them, and they have voluntarily accepted to serve in the reserve to those who are the regular forces.

The Canadian Tories believe that Americans will never invade Canada, and that if they were ever to do, they would welcome them to defend their own property and the interests of the Crown, and they don't believe the French will ever help America. To that effect, they attempt to challenge them to do their worst and to get rich on the backs of those who chose the party of liberty, and put on them the most undignified sufferance and forced them to labor in the service of the King until exhausted to death.

On the other hand, the Clergy, who is supported by the British rulers, makes it a point of glory to severely tyrannize those they consider to be rebels and refuse to be in their company, at the exception of three Jesuits, two regular priests who are, Father LaBrosse, Father Floquette, Father Germain, Father Trutau, parish priest of Kamouraska, Mr. Gacien, parish priest of Lotbinière, all gentlemen who have behaved according to their standing.

The Indians of Canada in favor of the Americans. There are only five who are Tories from the village of Saint-François, but who would not obey the Canadian Tories if they were not forced, and to follow their dictates against their own will.

The General is Mr. Harguiman and his Aide de Camp is Mr. De Lanoyer. The Governor is Mr. Cramahé; Mr. Canot is the one who set up the code for the distribution of orders and their executions with unimaginable cruelties. The names of the judges are Mr. Dunn, Maban, William, Panet, and Mr. Boisvert clerk. The wheat is three shillings and a half to four shillings.

There are parishes which have been disarmed and others not. Some say that they have been ordered to disarm and other say no. What is certain is that the parishes west of Quebec City have been entirely disarmed, but it was done by the Captains, doing it on their own without general orders.

The Canadians who support America, which is the majority, are very worried. They would like to join the Americans, but their fear that the Americans will not succeed in helping them prevents them from coming out openly. There are rumors to the effect that the news of their liberation is false, that they are being duped with false hopes, and that the Americans are not supported by the Canadians as much as they think. However, the joy they get at the news that France is joining America gives them a good idea of how America can succeed.

Also appended are the following observations by Capt. Joseph Travisie:

After arriving in Canada, Captain Travisie made a reconnaissance up to Sorel and he reported back that the English have built seventy houses for their troops and two sheds of a hundred feet in length each for their provisions, and that they have built entrenchments on both shores including fortifications.

A Mr. Dépin told him that the word is circulating about an order of a hundred and fifty carts with fifty boats that had been commandeered to carry ammunitions. Also, two brigades of six hundred men have left Sorel in the direction of Saint-Jean, no one knows why. However, it was also confirmed to him that fifty wounded Englishmen, no one knows from where, had been brought to Montreal. People say the two brigades have been deployed as reinforcement.

At Saint-François, there are only forty regular troops to mount guard. As for Saint-Antoine-Abbé, Nicollet, Yamachiche, Pointe du Lac, and Trois–Rivières, they have only a five hundred men regiment led by Colonel Bernard.

Captain Travisie was also given the names of the Voyageurs who led the Indians that the English had asked to come from the Michelmakina Algonquin tribe (misimikkinak, Lake Michigan Western Algonquin term meaning "big turtle.") to attack the Americans. But, when the Indians were taken to Montréal, General Harguiman did not see fit to use them. He was told that since the English had brought them there to make war they had replied that if they had to make war, they would do it against anyone but not against Americans, that that they would rather make war against them [the English] unless the seven hundred Indians that came were paid one hundred dollars each and were brought back to their village. The English tried to persuade them by force, but the Indians started to kill three of four of them. They would have destroyed them all throughout Montreal if, in order to appease them, the English had not decided to lavish them with presents and give them all they wanted in order to get rid of them as soon as possible. The same Voyagers assured them that the Illinois Indians were taken, and the Detroit and the traveling conditions from Michelmakina to the Detroit was not accessible.

Father Germain who is the parish priest of Saint-François, told him that he was convinced that the fortification the English were building in Sorel was simply to make believe that they were doing their best to protect Canada and justify the expense in the eyes of the King. But, that they were ready to abandon all of this as soon as they saw the Americans coming.

Finally, Mr. Lagrave, a merchant from Three Rivers, said he saw all of the cannons stationed at Saint-Jean being loaded onto ships and that they were being shipped to London.

APPENDIX - THE ISSUE OF AMERICA'S MANIFEST DESTINY TODAY

The following is the transcript of a live Internet video webcast conducted by Democratic Presidential pre-candidate Lyndon LaRouche, from the Wyndham Hotel in Billerica, Massachusetts. The thesis herein contained guided Professor Beaudry in his historical research and was originally published in Executive Intelligence Review vol. 27, number 4, January 2000.

Lyndon LaRouche in 2009

Thank you very much. I've chosen to do this in New England for a number of reasons. First of all, because the issue of Manifest Destiny as a debate over the foreign policy of the United States, is the leading issue today. The currents, the opposing currents on that debate at the end of the last century, and at the beginning of this century, those issues remain today more important than ever before.

And they're more important than ever before because we're in one of the worst crises worldwide we've seen in any recent century. And this policy has to be understood. Unfortunately, very few candidates who are running for President, have even the glimmer of ideas of what this means. Most American citizens no longer know what the issue is, or what its practical implications are. And tonight, I will attempt to make that, in a shortened version, clear to you.

This is New England, a good place to choose for dealing with this, because it was here in New England, as defined in 1630 by John Winthrop, the founder of New England, otherwise known as the Massachusetts Bay

Colony at that time, that the foundations of the states of Massachusetts, Maine, New Hampshire, Vermont, Connecticut, and Rhode Island were made, under the leadership of Winthrop and those associated with him.

From that point on, there was a certain policy about the developing of a nation in North America, starting from the Massachusetts Colony. That policy has continued as a viable policy to the present day.

It did not, however, start entirely here. It was a concept which was brought to North America by Europe. It was a policy which, in one form or the other, already dominated the late Fifteenth Century, the so-called century of the Renaissance. And, it was from the Renaissance that the ideas of our present, or what should be our present foreign policy, and what it has been in the best times in the past, was founded--from those ideas.

From the time of the Roman Empire, from the time of the birth of Christ, civilization in the Mediterranean region had collapsed, degenerated, and continued in a degenerate form of one degree or another, for about fifteen centuries.

But with the birth of Christ and the leadership role of his Apostles, there was a new conception of man and society, which was based largely upon the foundations of the Classical Greek tradition, especially the ideas associated with the work of Plato. And in the Apostles, especially in the Gospel of St. John, or the Epistles of Paul, you'll find this conception of man on which our later foreign policy here was founded. You'll find it established there; especially, for example, in Paul's Epistle in I Corinthians, Chapter 13, where this concept of man was set forward.

The Power of Cognition and the Golden Renaissance

But the idea is that man is not an animal. Man, unlike any other species, is capable of willfully increasing our species' power in and over the universe. This is possible, because we have a power which is called, technically, cognition, the power to discover universal physical and other principles, to prove that those principles are correct, and to apply those principles in ways which enable us to increase man's power in and over the universe, and to improve the conditions of life of the human being.

This quality in the person, the quality of cognition, combined with a determination to do good--in the sense of increasing man's power in the universe, in the sense of improving the conditions of life of human beings through the use of this power--was called, in the Ancient Greek, agape⁻, which is the term which was the subject of the original Greek version of Paul's I Corinthians, notably I Corinthians 13.

For a long period of time, almost fourteen centuries from the birth of Christ, there was a struggle by Christians, to establish a society which was consistent with that principle. That is, that all men and women are equally made in the image of the Creator, by virtue of having this power of cognition, the quality of agape⁻, the potential to increase man's power in and over the universe, and to improve the conditions of life through the discovery of these kinds of principles, which no animal could do.

And thus, we must have a society fit-a form of society fit, for that quality of creature: man cast in the image of the Creator. And it was only in the Fifteenth Century, in a period called the Golden Renaissance, that the first successful steps were made to actually establish this kind of society, for which people had struggled and dreamed over the intervening fourteen centuries.

This developed in the middle of the Fifteenth Century, around an event which is called the Council of Florence. But the enemies--the Roman feudal tradition, tried to stop the emergence of this form of society, which we call today the sovereign nation-state. And therefore, powerful forces, centered in Venice, organized a revolt against the efforts to form this kind of society.

The first such nation-states based on this principle, were France under Louis XI; and following that, modelled on the success of Louis XI in France, Henry VII in England founded the first modern nation-state in England, though his son and successor, Henry VIII, as we all know, erred. He stepped in the wrong direction a few times. He had a Monica Lewinsky in his life.

So, as a result of the struggle in Europe--and remember, Europe was dominated, from about 1517 until the middle of the Seventeenth Century, that is, 1648, by religious wars. Those who opposed the nation-state in Europe, tried to defend the old feudal order, in one way or another, by pitting parts of Europe against each other in religious wars. And terrible religious wars dominated Europe during most of the Sixteenth Century and the first half of the Seventeenth Century, until the Treaty of Westphalia.

A New Nation-State in North America

Now, it was under these conditions that people in England and elsewhere, conceived of establishing a new nation-state on the continent of North America. The first such venture was the founding of New England, by that name, by John Winthrop, in 1630. And it's from that, that the United States came.

Now, Massachusetts was not always good; New England was not always good. It deteriorated. But nonetheless, what was done under the leadership of Winthrop, and collaborators of his, such as the Mather family, in education and so forth, this was the foundation of what was continued by Benjamin Franklin during the Eighteenth Century, in leading this nation, or what became this nation, to founding the United States.

At a later point, the question came up, and it came up around the question of the Constitution in the 1780s, and in 1789 in particular: What was the mission, and what was the purpose by which we, as a nation, should define ourselves? How should we define our relations to other nations, in particular, but to the world in general? What was our purpose and our mission, which would be a kind of--our law, as it pertained to what purpose would guide us, in dealing with other parts of the world?

Now, back in the Fifteenth Century again, a crisis erupted. The Venetian oligarchy, which is a financier oligarchy, organized the fall of Constantinople, and turned Constantinople over to the Turkish or the Ottoman dynasty, thus dividing Europe, cutting Europe apart, and obstructing the development of the spread of nation-states which had been planned throughout Europe, nation-states such as--pioneer nation-states, such as France under Louis XI, or England under Henry VII.

And at that point, still in the Fifteenth Century, one of the founders of the Council of Florence, one of the organizers of it, Nicholas of Cusa, with his friends, launched an alternative to the Ottoman conquest of Constantinople, to try to save civilization as a whole, and European civilization in particular, by colonization, by voyages of exploration--by finding allies behind the back of the Ottoman Empire.

So, a map was drawn, drawn by one of the associates of Cusa, a geometer--who drew a map of the spherical Earth. This map was drawn by Toscanelli. The map went to Portugal. It was a map which influenced the Portuguese, in exploring the Atlantic, and going into the Indian Ocean.

The same map was picked up by Christopher Columbus, who had a correspondence with Toscanelli. And Christopher Columbus went to a woman, Isabella I of Spain, who was a little bit better than her husband, and much better than those who followed her as the rulers of Spain. And she sponsored Columbus's voyage to America, using the map to rediscover the continent on the other side of the Atlantic. And he succeeded.

And therefore, we had a Spanish development in the Americas, where people who didn't like the conditions of life in Spain and who had some courage, would flee to the Americas, to the so-called Hispanic Americas, to establish what became the foundations of nations in Central America and South America, that is, the Spanish-speaking part of this world.

At a later point, at the beginning of the Seventeenth Century, you had the great effort of John Winthrop to found New England, as the germ of a new nation, a new kind of sovereign nation-state republic, based on those principles, and to spread that. From that time on, from 1630, the patriotic Americans, who were dedicated to that heritage, including, typically, Benjamin Franklin, worked to develop the United States, or what became the United States, as a nation, to move westward, and to move toward Asia.

And the struggles: beginning with the King Philip's Wars here in New England, where the British and French tried to stop the spread of the Massachusetts Bay Colony, by organizing what was called King Philip's Wars, to stop the spread of the colony.

Other efforts were made. But nonetheless, the struggle went on. The struggle was always--colonize westward. Bring the best people from Europe, the best common people who believed in this idea; bring them to this land, develop this land, move westward, open the way to the west, keep moving westward.

This continued. Of course, in the middle of the Nineteenth Century, you had the great effort of Lincoln and others, to build a Transcontinental Railroad, to spread and develop this land, by building railways which would enable us to conquer the land, to make it open to the people.

Remember, the railways were actually development areas. Where a railroad went, on both sides of the railroad, you developed farms, you developed industries, you developed towns. You developed the land. You brought people in, people from Germany, from other parts of Europe, to settle and build farms, and spread the area under development.

U.S. Technology was a Model

And then we came to the West Coast. So, in 1861 to 1876, under Lincoln's leadership, and his followers, immediate followers, the United States emerged as the most powerful single economy in the world, the most advanced technologically. Not necessarily the most advanced scientifically, but the most advanced technologically.

Our level of technology was a model, so that by about 1876-1877, the entire world was looking to the United States as the model to be emulated. Russia adopted the model of the Americas. We had Mendeleyev, who was at the 1876 Philadelphia celebration of the Centennial of the founding of the United States. He went back to Russia, and he built the Trans-Siberian Railroad.

You had developments in Germany. Germany, in 1877, changed its policy fundamentally, so that the German economic policy was a copy of the American economic policy.

Japan in the 1870s, adopted the American model of Henry Carey. And Henry Carey directly had a hand in directing Japan in doing that, to lay the foundations of what became the economic successes in Japan. And the same thing happened with Sun Yat-sen at a later point.

Sun Yat-sen was a Chinese who was educated in Hawaii. While educated in Hawaii, he became the future founder of the nation of China as a republic. He was backed by the Americans. He was hated by the British, and persecuted by the British.

But if you look at the plans for the development of China by Sun Yat-sen, in a book which is published--we republished a copy of this book, even in China, to get it back-translated into Chinese, for the benefit of the Chinese. His model for the development of China, was the model of the United States, the model of 1861-1876: the American model.

A Great Debate

So in this period, there came a great debate, a debate between the patriots and traitors of the United States, particularly in the latter part of the century.

The patriots of the United States looked at the Pacific Ocean, and said, in continuation of the ideas of Cusa, that we must go across the Pacific, to help the nations of Asia develop.

And they understood something more about this. They understood that the culture of European civilization--when we speak of European civilization, we're talking about, essentially, a Greek-founded, or Classical

---

Greek foundation for European civilization, in all its achievements. So, it was a Christian matrix imposed upon the Greek Classical model. This was the model upon which our Constitution was based, our laws. This is the difference between us, and the British laws and the British traditions. That we recognized that we dealt in the world with other cultures: the culture of China, the culture of India.

That we, being the products of European Christian civilization, must find our way to come to an ecumenical agreement and cooperation with people of other cultures in other parts of the world.

And the great drive, and the great debate in the last part of the Nineteenth Century, between the patriots, on the one side, like Blaine from Maine, who was Secretary of State for a while, who was an associate of President Garfield, an associate of the great heroes of our nation in that period, had this conception: We must go across the Pacific to establish an ecumenical relationship and bond with the peoples on the other side of the Pacific Ocean, to develop the world as a whole for our common benefit. And we must reach out to other nations.

Democratic Reform in a Feudal System

If you look at European governments and European political systems, the political systems of Europe are, at their best, inferior to the form of government which we established here in the United States, with our Constitution.

What's the difference? We have- our head of state is an elected President. There is no person, under our law- of course, the Congress doesn't obey the law too much, too well these days- but there's no person under our law, who has greater authority in the state as a person, as an elected official, than the President of the United States. That is the characteristic of our Constitution.

Now, what's the difference, in Europe? With the exception of what de Gaulle tried to do with the Fifth Republic in France- which was an abortive effort, because when he went out of power, the Fifth Republic degenerated--European governments are not true republics. There has never been a true republic in Europe, not since the Greeks at least, or since the efforts in the Fifteenth Century.

Why? What happened in Europe, is, under the impact of the American Revolution, the idea of freedom received a jolt, and there were continuing efforts in the late part of the Eighteenth and in the Nineteenth Century, to develop republics in Europe. But the Europeans never succeeded in building a republic.

What they built was something different. They built movements which moved for democratization, to democratize society. And thus, what they did, is they put pressure on the existing form of government--which was a feudal form of government, based on a monarchy, or somebody who took the place of a monarch, a permanent bureaucracy, which stayed no matter what the government was otherwise, and a parliament.

Now, the parliament was a feudal institution. It was not a republican institution. And always, as you can see, if you look at the history of European governments, the monarch, the king, or the bureaucracy as such, could overthrow the parliament at any time they wanted to. All they would do is form a parliamentary crisis, and they'd dump the government.

So the government had no real power. The government had power to lobby, to pressure the state, to pressure those who rule society. But no power to actually make policy- power to help shape policy, power to pressure.

So, what we had in Europe was a democratic reform in a feudal system. And that's what the governments of Europe are to the present day. Look at the way their governments function. They are not true republics.

We are the only true republic, in that sense. We are the ones who bear this principle. So it was understood by the best people in our society: two things.

First of all, that what we are did not come from the ground in the United States. It did not come "from the frontier" as such. It did not come from barrooms on the frontier, or from cowboys and Indians shooting each other, which is what Teddy Roosevelt thought it came from, or said it came from. But he was a great liar, so you can never believe what he said anyway.

But the United States, as a republic, came from the greatest thinkers of Europe, typified by people like John Winthrop; typified by others who came here, and brought the best ideas of Europe here, with the hope that on this ground, those ideas could grow up and flourish as they had not been able to grow up and flourish in the same degree in Europe.

For example, in the end of the Eighteenth Century, the United States, our republic, was called a "temple of liberty and beacon of hope for all mankind." And our function as a nation-state, as something produced here through the best influence of the best ideas of European civilization, was to create a form of society which would be an inspiration and a friend to all humanity, in bringing forth on this planet, a system of sovereign nation-states, which would cooperate, for their mutual benefit, in an ecumenical way.

The Principle of Reason

Now, what does "ecumenical" mean in this sense?

You have a whole history of ecumenicism, particularly in the Mediterranean region, because you had, first of all, Judaism and Christianity. And you had the great Jewish writer– rabbi, as he's called, Philo of Alexandria, who was a friend of the Apostle Peter, and who wrote very important writings, who actually helped to civilize the Jewish religion at that point, which had been a captive of Babylon and the Romans at that time. And he laid down a principle of ecumenicism.

Later in the Fifteenth Century, the same Nicholas of Cusa to whom I referred, wrote a paper called De Pace Fidei, or The Peace of Faith, which has a dialogue among Christians, Jews, and Muslims, on what the relations must be among the people who represent these different religions.

What is the common basis to avoid religious war, and to have a peace among the faiths, based on the adoption of certain common principles? It's the same principle of Christianity. We call it the principle of reason.

In fact, if we can discover the truth, if we can discover a principle of nature, what we call a "universal physical principle," if we can prove that principle to be valid, demonstrate it to be universally valid, then we'd know, by the power we have to make that discovery, there's something going on in our minds which is not formal logic: the power of reason.

What we say, therefore, if we have a difference with others on religion, or on culture, we say that we must reason together, we must use this power of cognition, the principles which are made known to us through this sharing of this power of cognition, to recognize whatever our differences are in a particular faith as a given faith, that we must work together on the basis of reason. We must reason together, find a true universal principle, adopt it commonly, and work together on the basis of reason.

Civil society must not be a religious society, but civil society must be of an ecumenical form, based on this principle of reason. And that is the way that we will have to deal with cultures such as China, or the culture of India, or other cultures which come from roots other than European civilization. In the case of European or Mediterranean civilization, in dealing with Christianity, Judaism, and Islam, you don't have a great--you have problems and struggles, but you shouldn't have them, but because of a common root, you have an easier task in coming together in adopting common principles.

Whereas, you go into other parts of the world, you don't have the same cultural background. Therefore, you must look deeper, to the principle of reason, to find a common foundation for working together for a common interest. But it must be a voluntary association, based on reason teaching us that this is the thing we must do together, and civil society must be based on that.

For example, I referred recently in things we've published to one of our heroes, Moses Mendelssohn. Moses Mendelssohn in Germany, in the middle of the Eighteenth Century, played a key part in creating what is the modern Classical German culture. Now, you might say Classical German culture is a Jewish conspiracy. And in a sense, it was. And he was part of it. He was also the great liberator of Judaism from persecution, by these ideas.

One of his most famous writings, was on this subject. He remained, to his death, an Orthodox Jew. And he said he would, always. But, he said at the same time, society must be based on the principle of reason: Political society, civil society, must be based on the common principle of reason.

We Must Dedicate Ourselves to the Truth

And that we in the United States in particular, must exemplify that, the principle of reason. Not religious bigotry, but the principle of reason: that if something is true, we can discover the truth, and we can test it as to which is true and which is false, in universal principles.

And other than that, we must dedicate ourselves to the truth, even when we don't yet know it. That is, if we don't know what the answer is, we can at least dedicate ourselves to the urge and desire and method of finding the truth. And that's what our society is based on.

So, the conception among all the greatest thinkers of American politics, was in that direction. They may have said something slightly different than what I've just said, but we would all agree, among us. If they were alive and standing here today, we would agree. And Blaine would agree, even though I have some differences with some of the things Blaine said. But we would agree.

And the function of this nation is to be, still, to become again, the beacon of hope and temple of liberty for mankind, which it's not right now. Not even for our own citizens. For the 80% in the lower income bracket, it's not.

But it must become that again. That's our purpose. That's the function we have among nations. That's the role that the President of the United States must have, in dealing with other nations, in leading this nation, in his negotiations with other powers: to come to those forms of collaboration and agreements which are consistent with that.

We must call ourselves that, we must see ourselves as that, and we must function to that effect. We're not doing it now.

What is the Situation Now?

We're producing less and less

We're in a terrible situation. Not only is the United States in an economic crisis--and if we weren't stealing from other countries, we'd know how bad our poverty is. The United States is using its power and the power of the British Commonwealth combined, to steal massively from other nations.

For example, you wouldn't have the boom on Wall Street, unless, for the past 14 years, the United States had been looting Japan. We have been stealing from Japan. Japan is printing money, and issuing it, at a quarter-percent interest overnight. This money, Japanese yen, which are being issued by the Bank of Japan at a quarter-percent interest, are being borrowed by Americans and by Europeans, and others. They convert them into dollars; they use the yen to buy dollars. Then they come into our markets, and they jack the markets up, with financial speculation, like this great Internet bubble that's now ready to pop.

In this country, we have a deficit, a national so-called current account deficit, that we as a nation, are spending $300 to $400 billion a year more than we are taking in. We are taking that money, from other countries.

We are living, not on what we produce, but- we produce less and less. We're living upon slave labor, or virtual slave labor, from other countries. We don't produce our goods- or less and less. We get cheap goods from other countries, through virtual slave labor abroad. And our companies buy those cheap goods, and dump those things on us. And that's how we get along.

Look at our supermarket malls, for example. They're disgusting. No decent goods. Look at the fact that our satellites don't go up regularly, because they don't work so well anymore, because our engineers and our firms are no longer as competent as they used to be, because we're not a productive nation any more.

Our farmers, generally, the real farmers, the family farmers, are going bankrupt. When farmers who are now in their 60s and 70s die off, what's going to happen to the farms? There are no replacements for them, except cheap labor working on company farms. Gone.

Where are our industries? Look at New Hampshire, for example. How do people in New Hampshire live? We used to have industries here. We used to have respectable industries. We used to have some farming here, to get by. It was always a rather poor state, relative to Massachusetts, but a proud state. We used to make jokes when I lived up here, about the Massachusetts drivers and things like that.

But it was that kind of- we were proud. But we had some dignity. Now, we take in people's laundry. New Hampshire lives by tourism in the summer, and tourism in the ski season. But New Hampshire overall, as an economy, is no longer a viable economy.

You look at what's happened to Massachusetts. The collapse of the industrial potential of this area, of the technological potential. It's being destroyed.

So, this is true of the United States as a whole. We are being a self-destroyed nation. And the bills are piling up. Since Carter, since the middle of the 1970s, our national debt has become a cancer. Our total indebtedness has become a cancer, which is about to crush us.

When Japan goes down, as it may soon, or when Russia goes down, or a combination, and Brazil goes down, Mexico goes down, Ecuador's already gone, there's a crisis building up in Europe, we will go down too. And you will have people who are now in the upper 20% of income brackets, working as middle management at $60,000, $70,000 a year, with stock option bonanzas, which they're using to buy $300-400,000,

$600,000, million-dollar shacks, tar-paper shacks with Hollywood frontages on them, shacks that will collapse if people don't stay inside to keep the walls straight--this terrible stuff.

The Danger of Fascism

This is what we face. We can have the white shirts turn into brown shirts very easily in this country. You have people who have no skills, really, who are middle management, who are generally psycho-managers more than goods managers. And when they lose their jobs, when the Internet bubble collapses--not all the Internet industries will go down. But some of them are just fly-by-night operations, essentially. And when they go down, these people- who have got $600,000 to a million-dollar mortgages on these tar-paper shacks, with a little bit of glorification and fancy faucets- when they go down, those mortgages will be unpayable. They'll be migrating, looking for a job, and we're going to have panic in this country, not so much among the people who are already poor, because they've gotten used to poverty. But these people will go crazy.

And if we don't provide a solution for this problem here, a Roosevelt-style solution, we're going to have white shirts turn into brown shirts. And you're going to have the rage, which you see in the death-penalty cases, the finality rule in death-penalty cases, as in particularly Virginia and Texas, or now in Florida, where you've got the--both Bushes who want to kill everybody. I don't know, just for pleasure or what not? They might as well open a Roman circus, and just get 'em out there, and kill each other or something.

But a meanness in the American people, an absolute meanness. You turn that kind of thing loose, with the absolute lack of morality--as we

---

used to understand morality as morality, person to person--drive these people into a rage, and you're going to have the brown shirts, or their equivalent, stampeding through the society, destroying us, tearing us apart.

So, we have a crisis. Since last August, when the financial crisis, the Russian crisis hit, we've been getting into wars. It started with Al Gore and his friends.

Clinton had a problem with the Lewinsky case--actually, with the Starr Chamber. He was distracted. In the absence, while the President was distracted by this impeachment process from last summer on through February, Al Gore and his friends inside the administration began organizing wars, together with the British government.

You had the bombing of a pharmaceutical factory in Sudan. There was no reason to do that. They were not involved in terrorism, or producing something- It was done because Al Gore and Madeleine Half-bright wanted it done.

You had other incidents. You had Al Gore's fanatical speech, for example, in Kuala Lumpur, attacking the Prime Minister of Malaysia in a way that even a Nazi diplomat wouldn't have dared do in his time. Filthy behavior! The same crowd.

Then you had the forcing of the renewed bombing of Iraq, pushed through by Al Gore. Not the President. By Al Gore and his friends, Madeleine Half-bright and so forth.

Then you had us go into a no-win stupid war, organized by the same people, behind the back of the President, in the case of the so-called Kosovo war, or the war against Yugoslavia. The bombing war, which has simply destroyed the territory. It solved no problem. The conditions are far worse than when the war started, throughout the entire region, including Kosovo.

Now, the same forces, the heirs of Bush and Thatcher, have launched terrorists internationally, headquartered in London. They've launched it in Transcaucasia. They've launched wars between India and Pakistan, virtual wars, now ongoing, and similar things throughout the world.

So, you're in a situation which reminds you, in a sense, of what happened during the 1930s, during the period of the 1930s Depression.

But, at the same time that the economic situation is ready to blow, we've got this chaos- threat of wars. We have already the threat of a deflationary collapse: A 60-80% collapse of the stock market, for example, could occur at any time. Nobody knows when, because political factors will decide when and how things happen. We have a hyperinflationary tendency in real estate and elsewhere already building up, reminding us of Weimar Germany in 1923. They could go that way.

We've got wars and chaos spreading. We've got the two biggest dummies in politics, running as leading Presidential candidates of the Democratic and Republican parties. Either of these idiots in power, whether they're just dummies or not, is a threat to our national security. That's our situation.

Now, what's the solution? That means we're coming to a point in foreign policy, this financial system, this monetary system, this crazy thing that was started in 1971 with Nixon and the floating-exchange-rate system, this is about to come to an end, one way or another.

We're in a time in which the people who represent money, big money, are hysterical. Their plans are not to have Wall Street go up forever; you've got people who have bought into what they call "income streams"- people who have bought up raw materials, especially through London. The mega-mergers are grabs. They take all the money in sight, and they'll never pay the bills. But somebody behind the scenes, who is behind the money grab, who has an angle on grabbing those assets when these mega-merger organizations go bankrupt. This means gold mines, it means petroleum, it means the communications industry--which is being grabbed up now. The idea of the communications industry being indispensable--anybody who controls communications after the system goes belly-up, will be able to control that income stream as a monopoly, or as a syndicate that controls it as a monopoly.

And we have the same thing with our power system. We're running out of power. But people are moving, like Enron, to grab up power from companies, power companies that are going bankrupt, that control your energy.

Control communications, control energy, control food supplies, control raw materials, the things on which life depends: to control those things, means you control whatever income stream exists when the thing goes belly-up financially.

And they're already moving for it. They have the suckers who are still betting on Wall Street. They're still betting on these crazy stocks, betting on these financial ventures. They're counting on their mutual funds, their money-manager accounts. They think they're making money on it. They'll be wiped out.

We don't know exactly when, but it's coming. No. The smart guys are not doing that. They're letting the suckers do it, especially the suckers in the upper 20% of income brackets.

They're grabbing up, around the world--they're grabbing assets. Petroleum assets, mineral assets, communications system assets, power system assets, water assets, food monopoly assets. They're grabbing them up. And when the malls go bankrupt, when the suburban projects go belly-up, they'll be there, controlling the income stream and controlling the world. That's their idea. They're mad and greedy.

That would mean a New Dark Age. We've seen this before in human history, in European history in particular, this kind of thing. And if we don't stop it, don't prevent it, it's going to mean Hell, Hell on Earth, at least for decades to come.

We Have to Take Roosevelt-Style Decisions

So, what's the solution?

The solution is, of course, that we have to take Roosevelt-style decisions and answer the crisis. We have to act. We have to create a new monetary system. We have to put the thing into bankruptcy reorganization. We have to make sure that people don't die on the streets, because their pensions aren't paid, because their savings accounts have disappeared.

We've got to keep order, so normal life continues. We've got to improve employment and production. We've got to do those things as emergency actions immediately. We've got to prevent chaos and bring back order, and start to put ourselves back together again.

But we can't do it all by ourselves. We have to do it with other nations, or at least some other nations. Now, we need some other nations. Well, most of the world's population, where is it?

Most of the world's population is in Asia: India, Indonesia, Malaysia, other parts of Southeast Asia, Central Asia, China, Japan, Korea. And then, also Africa.

This is where the great part of the human population is. Then we have ruined areas of the world, which could be great and prosperous, with good labor forces, at least the remnants of them, in South and Central

America. Many of these countries have good labor forces, under good conditions.

So, we have people with whom we should cooperate and can cooperate, to put this planet in some kind of order.

And this brings us back to the question of Manifest Destiny. Does the United States still have the function, of being a temple of liberty and beacon of hope for these nations of the world? And can we do that by making sure we do it also internally, to restore the nation internally, as a temple of liberty and beacon of hope, in order to give it the moral authority to be a temple of liberty and beacon of hope worldwide?

Could it be done? Yes, it could be done.

A Proper Foreign Policy Approach

Let's take the case of my own, and Helga's, and our friends' foreign policy, which we've been practicing. This is not something we dreamed up, it's something we've been practicing.

It started in New Hampshire, in the New Hampshire primary campaign in 1980, when I was sitting at a table at a gun club event which had about 2,500 people up there in the Concord area, at what used to be the old New Hampshire Highway Hotel.

And because we were arranged at the table as Presidential candidates, in alphabetical order by surname, Ronald Reagan was at the end of the table, and I was next to him. And you had all these other funny fellows there, too.

So, Ronald and I got into a little bit of discussion. There wasn't much substance to it. It was just a discussion. But I saw, when he put his speech together, a five-minute speech which we were each allotted to do, I saw the way he did it, and realized the man was not as dumb as he was supposed to be. He had problems, but he wasn't stupid. And I recognized that from talking to him.

So, when he became President, or had been elected, I, as a Democrat, got into a conversation with some of the people who were going to form, who were in the process of forming the new administration. And I said, "Well, what's your agenda?" You know how politicians talk.

And a whole bunch of them, including Richard Richards, and so forth, said: "What's your agenda?"

So, I would discuss with these people the things that I thought the United States ought to do. And they would say, "We like that, we don't like that, we like that, we don't like that."

So, we would go around (Helga went with me to some of these meetings), and we'd meet various people, and we'd talk with the Democrats. I would say to the Democrats, leading Democrats in the Congress, "This is the way I think we ought to deal with the Reagan administration. We ought to move quickly, because there are some bad things over there. But we ought to move quickly to find common denominators which are good for the nation, and get this thing going in that direction now."

Well, one of the results was that at the end of 1981, I became--I had a project. And the question was discussing it with the Russians, or the Soviets then.

So, to make short of the thing, I got involved, on behalf of the Reagan administration, in discussing with the representatives of the top Soviet circles, on my policy for dealing with the weapons crisis and related matters. So that led, eventually, about a year later, to Reagan making the famous speech announcing his SDI, on March 23rd, 1983.

Now, that went awry afterward. And I was out of the picture soon, because the enemies of mine got into it pretty quick. And they made a mess of it. So what they're talking about, about missile defense systems today, is mostly nonsense. Even though there were some people in the background who knew what we were talking about.

But since that time, and in earlier businesses in dealing with non-aligned nations and developing nations generally, I've been pretty much involved with the question of foreign policy matters, over a period of about at least three decades. And I know a lot of people, if you look at some of my endorsements from various parts of the world, from leading figures from South America, Europe, Asian countries, and so forth, you see a reflection of the fact that I have been a significant figure on their horizon, in terms of relations with the United States and others, over this period of time.

And in many of these countries, there are people who wish I were President. They think it would be good for them and good for the world. And they say so.

A New Bretton Woods System

So, I know these countries. I know what we can do. And I know that if I were President, I could deal with this problem. The problem is, that we must have an emergency action to put the present monetary system, which isn't functioning, into bankruptcy, bankruptcy reorganization, by governments, by sovereign governments.

In other words, we all agree that each government will take its chunk of the problem, and they'll put that chunk through their own bankruptcy reorganization. But then we will coordinate our efforts, to get something out of this which will be stable for all of us.

Now obviously, if you're going to make a sudden move like that, you've got to base your move on something which is a proven precedent. You can't come up with some completely newfangled thing that nobody ever heard of before, and expect the people, as well as the politicians, to suddenly accept that as a plan of action.

You've got to say: "Here's where we went wrong. Here's where we were doing things that were working, relatively speaking, and here's where we went wrong and we began to do the wrong thing. That's why we're in a mess. Now, let's go back to the point in the road where we made the wrong turn, and let's begin to move from there."

So, this idea of a New Bretton Woods, is very simple. We had, from 1944 through '58, and somewhat beyond, we had, with all its faults, a monetary system and a general economic policy which worked. It may not have worked the way we liked it, but it worked, relative to anything we've seen since. We had recovery of the world from the war, economic recovery.

We had the Marshall Plan. We had a rebuilding of the United States economy, based largely upon Marshall Plan exports into Europe. So we built up our industries in helping Europe develop, and Japan develop, through Marshall Plan cooperation, and through that kind of policy; through the Bretton Woods agreements, the old Bretton Woods agreements: sovereign nation-state, gold reserve, fixed parities, tariffs which were protective for all countries, each and all countries, trade agreements of that type, and so forth. Low-interest, long-term loans to promote international trade, and that sort of thing.

It worked. With all the failures, it worked! With all the problems, it worked, relative to anything we've seen since 1971. If we had never stopped doing that, we wouldn't have the world financial and economic crises, or the U.S. crisis we have today.

So, it should be obvious to nations which have gone through this kind of experience of the present IMF system--they all know it doesn't work, they all know it's destroying us.

Well, let's get rid of it. Well, you don't ask one nation, by itself, to get rid of it. You try to get a group of nations together, to say, "We will jointly agree this thing has to go."

And if you have the majority of the human race in the deal with you, it's likely to fly. And if the United States is a partner in it, the President of the United States, it's likely to fly, particularly if the American people at that time perceive a major crisis which needs some fixing.

And our argument to the American people is: This is what worked. We've got the facts to prove it. You've got senior citizens who remember how it worked, who can remind you of it and tell you about it. That worked. What you're doing now, has failed.

Now, let's simply go back to the turn in the road where we made the wrong turn. Go back to the Bretton Woods model, maybe change the relations among states a bit, but do basically the same thing. Go in the same direction. Learn the lessons of the 1930s and 1940s and 1950s, and go back to that.

A National Mission

Now, what does that mean? As I dealt with this yesterday, in a press conference in Concord, where the question came up, particularly from one of our friends who is in the machine-tool area: How do we do this?

I said, "Well, you can't just have an economy and set up a master plan of how it's going to work and have it work. You've got to have a national mission. You've got to have a sense of purpose. What are you going to do? Where are you going to go?"

Well, the general condition of this planet is as follows. Presuming we've gone back to the old Bretton Woods model, or something like it, the same principles, the same general idea, now, how are we going to build our way globally out of the crisis? How are we going to have a mutual advantage: China, India, Indonesia, Malaysia, South America, Central America, Europe, the United States? How are we going to have a deal that is equitable to all? What do we have to do?

Well, the basic problem of the planet is that when Roosevelt died, we didn't do what he intended to do, that is, to rip up all vestiges of Portuguese, Dutch, British, and French colonialism and imperialism, and end the domination of this planet by a free-trade system. That was Roosevelt's intention, as he stated plainly and repeatedly, to Winston Churchill.

But, when Roosevelt died, Winston Churchill won. And the Washington gang took orders from Churchill, along with the people who worked for Churchill. And they put the policy in.

So, as a result of that, we did not address the question which Roosevelt intended to do, is to transform what had been the colonial region of the world, or semi-colonial, under free-trade domination and looting, and transform this into a collection of sovereign nation-state republics, which would be in partnership with the United States in particular, as well as Europe, and to try to build this world up so that you had just economic conditions throughout the world as a whole. To bring nations together as sovereign nation-states, so we would not create a situation where we'd look forward, in Roosevelt's view--and mine at the time, when I was in service- to a world where you wouldn't have another terrible world war.

And the way to do that, is to have a just economic system, and a just political system, in which sovereign nation-states have a partnership, a sovereign partnership, in terms of doing things together, which are in the common interest.

We Must Rebuild the Nation

Now, what does that mean today?

That means in countries like China, or India, or Southeast Asia, or South America now, Central America, you have nations which could not by themselves, with their own resources, recover in time to meet the desperate condition of all of their population.

One case is China. China has now currently a rate of growth, annual rate of growth, of about 7-8% per year, maybe 8.5. It depends on how you calculate.

But that sounds very good, considering the fact that the United States has no growth, really no net growth. You take the hot air out of our financial system, we are contracting, as manifest by the fact that we can no longer afford the health care we used to have. They tell us we can no longer afford the pensions we used to have, we can no longer have the educational system we used to have, we can no longer afford anything that we used to have.

So obviously, we've become much poorer. And anybody who's telling us that things have become better is kidding themselves, or blowing hot air, blowing bubbles, as they're doing on Wall Street.

So, it's not enough to have a certain rate of growth, you've got to be able to sustain the growth. Now, you can have growth in the inland area of

China, for example, where very poor people live. The Chinese economy is mostly located on the coastal areas, or near the coast, traditionally.

Inland, it's poor, very poor, desperately poor. They're one of the poorest parts of the world. They're just better organized than some other parts of the world. But they're very poor.

And the social stability of China, depends not merely on improving the economic conditions of these people, but improving the cultural conditions; and the improvement in economic conditions, is necessary to improve cultural conditions. That means you have to have a higher standard of living, more education, and all the things that go with that.

Well, they're not going to be able to do that, without a lot of high technology. You cannot sustain growth at high rates, without also increasing the average productive powers of labor, as measured in physical terms.

We can do that. We have on this planet the ability to produce the technologies, which, used by developing countries such as China, or India, or South American countries, or Africa, we have the technologies, which, on the long term, will enable these countries to sustain growth, real growth, on a stable basis.

Ah! We used to be machine-tool exporters. We used to be high-technology exporters. Europe, especially continental Europe, used to be high-technology exporters. Present-day Russia has some industries, the scientific, military and scientific-industrial complex, which could produce machine tools--capable of doing it.

Japan has a Machine-tool Capability.

If we, the nations which have a machine-tool type of capability for science-driver machine-tool development--we can supply the developing sector of the world with the tools and the technology which they need, to increase their productive powers of labor, per capita and per square kilometer. That solves their problem.

We need to employ our people. We need to get back to work. What should we do?

We should build those industries, and farms, and so forth; we need to maintain our own national economic security at home.

But what should we export? What should we concentrate on, in terms of exports? We should concentrate, together with Europe, together with Japan, and other countries which have a high-technology capability, on building up--what? Our universities, particularly science education. Our university laboratories, which test discovery and development of scientific principles; our machine-tool capabilities, including the highly specialized ones, and develop the new principles, including the ones that produce the applications for sophisticated machine tools, including the mass production machine tools that go with that.

And helping these countries get also the supporting repair capabilities and maintenance capabilities, in the area where the industries are developing, which they don't have in these countries now, at least not adequately.

That should be our mission, particularly for the next quarter-century, next 30 years. We should rebuild ourselves, not only to put our own shop at home in repair, but to orient ourselves, using this aerospace industry as a focal point or driver for this thing, to retool the United States with a mission.

We, together with other countries which can do this, are going to adopt a mission of helping the rest of the world transform itself to end this kind of deprivation and misery, which affrights us and disgusts us. And thus we, those nations and we, should be able to meet together to come to the kind of terms which will be durable, because they'll be beneficial over a long period of time to come. We have to understand our Manifest Destiny.

The Role of Legitimate Government

Our Manifest Destiny lies in Classical Greek civilization, its unique contribution to global civilization. It lies in the role of Christianity, especially the Apostles, like John and Paul, in taking this Greek Classical legacy, and using this as the tool of Christianity, to improve the condition of mankind, as the Renaissance did later.

We need to develop the nation-state, the idea that a national government has no moral authority, except as it is founded on an absolute commitment to promote and defend the General Welfare of all of its people, including their posterity.

That's the only right that a government has to rule. Otherwise, it's simply some group of people that treats the government and the people as their personal property, and passes down laws accordingly.

But the only foundation for law, is the principle of the General Welfare: that all human beings are equally made in the image of the Creator. It is our obligation to promote their General Welfare so defined, as creatures of cognition and reason, to develop and cultivate their powers of cognition and reason, to develop all children, to develop all adults, equally, and call that the General Welfare. To improve the condition of the present and future generations, the General Welfare. That is the only moral authority and the chief responsibility of legitimate government.

Our concern is to have on this planet the emergence of governments which correspond to this principle of the General Welfare, which is the foundation of law in the Preamble of our Constitution, and of our constitutional law. And to make that commitment, define that, our being the temple of liberty, make that the definition of our being a beacon of hope. And let us reach out to other nations, with that message, with that commitment, with that purpose, and say, "Let's end this nonsense. Let's learn the lesson. Let's deal with the crisis."

And let us, in the process, to show this is no novel idea, let us understand the Greek Classic. Let us understand the mission of the Apostles. Let us understand the accomplishments of the Fifteenth-Century Renaissance. Let us understand the achievements of the great scientists and others who struggled to make the Renaissance possible, including Abelard and Charlemagne, or Dante Alighieri and others who came before that, who made it possible.

What it Means to be an American

Let us remember that, and let them live in us. This is no wild idea. We are simply affirming the proven principles of history, and the history of the United States in particular. Let us project that. Let us encourage our children, our citizens, to project that. When they say, "What are you?" You're an American citizen. What does that mean? Other countries have citizens. What do you mean by your being an American citizen? What does it mean? What's your mission, what's your commitment? What's your standard for picking the politicians you elect? What do you demand and expect them to do? Where do you expect them to stand? On some bite-size slogan they put out? Some phony gimmick, some sideshow, boola-boola, or do you want someone who thinks like that, who you can trust, because they are committed to that?

To educate our children, so that when they reach maturity, they're that kind of a person, where each person can finally see themselves in what I call the simultaneity of eternity. Not an unusual term, but one rarely used.

That once we understand our nature, we understand that we are made in the image of the Creator, each equally so. We must cultivate or redeem that quality which is within us, given to us at birth. We must relive the acts of reason, the discovery of universal principle, which has been passed down to us, for us to re-experience and absorb in ourselves.

We are short-lived. We are born, and we shall die, all of us. Then, what is the meaning of our life, as our human life? Is it not to assimilate and cultivate in ourselves, those qualities which define us as human; to absorb the gifts of reason from preceding generations, from history; to utilize those and preserve and defend those gifts of reason, to add something to that for future generations, so that when we pass on, we have retained a permanent place in the span of eternity?

That is the natural capability, and also the right of every human being: not to be an animal that is born and dies, that has pleasure in the meantime. The right of every human being is to live in such a way, that they, in their own way, can have their powers of reason cultivated, can find something good to do for humanity, so that they can die with a smile on their face, because they die with the assurance that in the life they had, they have secured a permanent place, an identity for themselves, in the simultaneity of eternity.

That's the commitment we must have. That is, to spark what's inside us, and must radiate from us, so that we become a true Beacon of Hope and Temple of Liberty for all mankind. That's what all of my predecessors in this political profession, who were good people, thought and dreamed.

That's what Blaine, in his own way, from Maine dreamed. That's what John Winthrop, the founder of New England, dreamed. That's what Benjamin Franklin attempted to do. That's what Cotton Mather preached, and preached to others. That's what Lincoln represented. That's what Garfield represented. That's what McKinley represented.

That's what Cleveland didn't represent. That's what Wilson didn't represent. That's what Coolidge didn't represent.

That's what Roosevelt, in his own imperfect way, tried to represent. That's what poor Kennedy, who was assassinated, was groping to try to represent, too. All the best people at least tried to represent that, in their own way. And that, for us, as Americans, when we were good, was always, for us, our choice of Manifest Destiny. Thank you.

NOTES

Chapter One

[1] American Declaration of Independence.

[2] The American War of Independence, 1775-1783, The British Library, 1975, p.13.

[3] From Claude Bélanger, Department of History, Marianopolis College.

[4] Henry Gosselin, George Washington's French Canadian Spy, J.H. French Printing, Inc., Brunswick Me, 1998, p. 78.

[5] Graham Lowry, How The Nation Was Won, EIR, 1988, p. 440.

[6] Robert Coakley and Stetson Conn, The War of the American Revolution, Center for Military History, Washington DC, 2010, p.33-34.

[7] Michael P. Gabriel, Major General Richard Montgomery: the Making of an American Hero, FDU Press.

[8] Spy Letters of the American Revolution, Benedict Arnold to John André , July 15, 1780.

Chapter Two

[1] John Quincy Adams described in a most beautiful manner the purpose of his policy of Manifest Destiny with respect to the American Declaration of Independence. He wrote:

"In a conflict [of] seven years, the history of the war by which you maintained that Declaration, became the history of the civilized world...It was the first solemn declaration by a nation of the only legitimate foundation of civil government. It was the cornerstone of a new fabric, destined to cover the surface of the globe. It demolished at a stroke, the lawfulness of all governments founded upon conquest. It swept away all of the rubbish of accumulated centuries of servitude. From the day of this Declaration, the people of North America were no longer the fragment

of a distant empire, imploring justice and mercy from an inexorable master in another hemisphere. They were a nation, asserting as of right, and maintaining by war, its own existence. A nation was born in a day...It stands, and must forever stand, alone, a beacon on the summit of the mountain, to which all the inhabitants of the earth may turn their eyes for a genial and saving light...a light of salvation and redemption to the oppressed." - Quoted in Nancy Spannaus, Adams' Community of Principle: The Monroe Doctrine, EIR, November 16, 2007, p. 68.

[2] Letter from J.Q. Adams to J. Adams, St. Petersburg, August 31, 1811, in Writings, IV, p. 209. Italics added by Samuel Flagg Bemis, John Quincy Adams, and the Foundations of American Foreign Policy, New York Alfred A. Knopf, 1949, p. 182.

[3] Lyndon H. LaRouche Jr, *The issue of America's Manifest Destiny for today*, EIR, January 28, 2000.

[4] John Jay, *Journal of Continental Congress*, October 21, 1774.

[5] The Times Atlas of World History.

[6] Letters of Delegates to Congress: Volume 1, August 1774 – August 1775, Silas Deane to Samuel Adams, p. 262.

[7] *Journals of the Continental Congress*, 1774-1789, WEDNESDAY, OCTOBER 26, 1774. *To the inhabitants of Quebec.*

[8] Letter from J.Q. Adams to J. Adams, St. Petersburg, August 31, 1811, in Writings, IV, p. 209. Italics added by Samuel Flagg Bemis, John Quincy Adams, and the Foundations of American Foreign Policy, New York Alfred A. Knopf, 1949, p. 182.

[9] Lyndon H. LaRouche Jr, T*he issue of America's Manifest Destiny for today*, EIR, January 28, 2000.

[10] John Jay, *Journal of Continental Congress*, October 21, 1774.

[11] The Times Atlas of World History.

[12] Letters of Delegates to Congress: Volume 1, August 1774 – August 1775, Silas Deane to Samuel Adams, p. 262.

[13] Journals of the Continental Congress, 1774-1789, WEDNESDAY, OCTOBER 26, 1774. *To the inhabitants of Quebec.*

Chapter Three

[1] This is described in detail by Lyndon H. LaRouche Jr in the January 28, 2000 *The issue of America's Manifest Destiny for Today*, published in EIR.

[2] Francis Parkman, France and England in North America, Volume I, The Library of America, 1984, p. 1173.

[3] The Times Atlas of World History.

[4] Letters of Delegates to Congress: Volume 1, August 1774 – August 1775, Silas Deane to Samuel Adams, p. 262.

[5] American Declaration of Independence.

[6] See my two previous reports THE TRAGEDY OF THE Québec ACT OF 1774 and GO WEST YOUNG MAN!

[7] The Times Atlas of World History.

[8] Montesquieu.

[9] Journals of the Continental Congress, 1774-1789, WEDNESDAY, OCTOBER 26, 1774. To the Inhabitants of Québec.

[10] Henri Gosselin, George Washington's French-Canadian Spy. A clinical case study of breaking with the self-imposed shackles of public opinion, J.H. French Printing, Inc., Brunswick, Me 1998, 216 pages, p. 3.

[11] Henri Gosselin, Op. Cit., p. 1.

[12] Op. Cit., p. 110-11.

[13] Pierre Dufour and Gerard Goyer, Clement Gosselin, Dictionary of Canadian Biography.

[14] Letter to the Honorable Congress, Thomas Miffin, President, from Clément Gosselin, Capt., in Henry Gosselin, Op. Cit., p. 180.

[15] Henri Gosselin, Op. Cit., p. 214.

Made in the USA
Monee, IL
04 August 2022